Vest Pocket
GERMAN

Formerly published as: GERMAN IN A NUTSHELL

By
HENRY REGENSTEINER, Ph.D.
Department of Modern Languages
Brooklyn College

PUBLISHED BY

INSTITUTE FOR LANGUAGE STUDY
Westport, Connecticut 06880

DISTRIBUTED TO THE BOOK TRADE BY
HENRY HOLT & COMPANY

Library of Congress Cataloging-in-Publication Data

Regensteiner, Henry.
   Vest Pocket German.

   Previously published as: German in a Nutshell.
   1. German language—Conversation and phrase books—
English. 2. German language—Grammar—1950-
3. German language—Dictionaries—English. 4. English
language—Dictionaries—German. I. Title.
PF3121.R429   1989   438.3'421   89-15368
ISBN 0-8489-5103-4

Printed in the United States of America

HH Editions 9 8 7 6   0008-5

GETTING THE MOST OUT OF YOUR COURSE

THE WORLD is growing smaller every day. Far-sighted people who recognize the value of speaking a second language will reap the benefits of greater business success, more traveling enjoyment, easier study and finer social relationships.

VEST POCKET GERMAN will unlock for you the treasure house of learning a language the easy way, with a fresh, new approach—without monotonous drills. Before you know it, you'll be speaking your new language easily and without embarrassment. You will be able to converse with fascinating people from other lands and read books and magazines from their country in the original language.

Much research and painstaking study has gone into the "Vest Pocket" method of learning a new language as easily as possible. This Course is the result of that research, and for the reader's convenience it is divided into several basic, closely related sections:

The KEY TO PRONUNCIATION explains the sounds of the language. Each sentence is accompanied by the phonetic spelling to help you learn the pronunciation. This method has been tested extensively and is found to be the best to enable the student to associate sounds with written forms.

The BASIC SENTENCE PATTERNS are the unique new approach to sentence construction. Here you will find sentence patterns needed in general conversation. On these basic patterns you can build sentences to suit your own particular needs.

The EVERYDAY CONVERSATIONS form the main section of this book. Here you will find a large number of situations useful for general language learning and traveling purposes. You will learn hundreds upon hundreds of conversational sentences you may need to make yourself understood. Even more important, the material is organized to provide you with a wide basis for varying the vocabulary and sentences as much as your interest and ingenuity might desire.

The OUTLINE OF GRAMMAR provides a rapid understanding of the grammatical structure of your new language. The "Basic Sentence Patterns" are closely correlated with this section to give you a quick knowledge of the language.

The two-way DICTIONARY of over 6500 entries includes all the words used in the Everyday Conversations and contains another 3000 frequently used words and expressions. It thus forms a compact and invaluable tool for the student.

Here are the tools. Use them systematically, and before you know it you will have a "feeling" for the new language. The transcriptions furnish authentic reproduction of the language to train your ear and tongue to the foreign sounds; thus you can SEE the phrase, SAY the phrase, HEAR the phrase, and LEARN the phrase.

Remember that repetition and practice are the foundation stones of language learning. Repeat and practice what you have learned as often as you can. You will be amazed (and your friends will, too) how quickly you have acquired a really practical knowledge of German.

THE EDITORS

TABLE OF CONTENTS

KEY TO GERMAN PRONUNCIATION

Most sounds of German are easy for speakers of English to master. A few sounds not occurring in English have been presented in greater detail, with useful hints for their pronunciation. A careful reading of the following instructions will help you greatly in acquiring correct pronunciation.

VOWELS

The vowels in German are generally long when followed by an *h* in the same syllable and stressed, and also mostly when followed by a single consonant. Unstressed vowels are usually short.

GERMAN SPELLING	PHONETIC SYMBOL	DESCRIPTION	EXAMPLES
a (short)	a	As *a* in *father*, but short.	*packen* (pa'-kĕn), to pack
a (long), *aa, ah*	ah	As *a* in *father*.	*Vater* (fah'-tĕr), father *wahr* (vahr), true
e (short)	e	As *e* in *met*.	*Bett* (bet), bed
e (long), *ee, eh*	eh	As *e* in *they* or *a* in *fate*, but without any diphthongal glide.	*Feder* (feh'-dĕr), pen *Meer* (mehr), sea *Ehre* (eh'-rĕ), honor
e	ĕ	Unstressed *e* as in *sufferer*.	*verlangen* (fĕr-lang'-ĕn), to desire
i (short)	i	As *i* in *fit*.	*bitte* (bi'-tĕ), please
i (long), *ie, ih, ieh*	ee	As *i* in *machine*.	*Maschine* (ma-shee'-nĕ), machine *mieten* (mee'-tĕn), to rent *ziehen* (tsee'-ĕn), to pull

7

GERMAN SPELLING	PHONETIC SYMBOL	DESCRIPTION	EXAMPLES
o (short)	o	As o in obey, or better as o in north, but very short.	kommen (ko'-měn), to come
o (long), oo, oh	oh	As o in rose, but without the diphthongal glide sound of w as in English.	Rose (roh'-zě), rose Boot (boht), boat Rohr (rohr), tube
u (short)	u	As u in put or oo in book.	Mutter (mu'-těr), mother
u (long), uh	oo	As u in rule.	Buch (bookh), book Uhr (oor), watch
y	i	Usually as short German i (see above), but may also be pronounced as short ü (see "Vowels with Umlaut").	Typistin (ti-pi'-stin or tü-pi'-stin) typist Typus (tü'-pus), type

VOWELS WITH *UMLAUT*

The graphic sign called *Umlaut* (literally "sound transformer") consists of two dots (¨) placed over the vowels *a*, *o* and *u* to indicate a change in pronunciation of these vowels, which is achieved by rounding the lips in pronouncing them, except in the case of *a–ä*. The *Umlaut* may be replaced by an *e* following the vowel (e.g. *ue* instead of *ü*), which is done especially when an entire word is written in capitals or when the first letter of a sentence or a noun is a vowel with *Umlaut* (e.g. *Ueber* instead of *Über*).

GERMAN SPELLING	PHONETIC SYMBOL	DESCRIPTION	EXAMPLES
ä (short)	e	As short German e.	ertränken (er-treng'-kěn), to drown
ä (long), äh	eh	As long German e.	Fähre (feh'-rě), ferry-boat
ö (short)	ö	As e in met, but with the lips rounded, or approximately as u in but.	göttlich (göt-licн), divine
ö (long), öh	öh	As long German e, but with the lips rounded.	höflich (höhf'-licн), polite Höhe (höh'-ě), height

GERMAN SPELLING	PHONETIC SYMBOL	DESCRIPTION	EXAMPLES
ü (short)	*ü*	As short German *i*, but with the lips rounded.	*füllen* (fü'-lĕn), to fill *Mütter* (mü'-tĕr), mothers
ü (long), *üh*	*üh*	As long German *i*, but with the lips rounded.	*müde* (müh'-dĕ), tired *rühren* (rüh'-rĕn), to stir

DIPHTHONGS

A diphthong is a combination of vowel sounds pronounced as one unit. German diphthongs are slightly shorter than English diphthongs.

GERMAN SPELLING	PHONETIC SYMBOL	DESCRIPTION	EXAMPLES
ei, ai (*ey, ay*)	*ī*	As *i* in *mine*.	*rein* (rīn), pure *Hai* (hī), shark
au	*ou*	As *ou* in *house*.	*Haus* (hous), house
eu, äu	*oi*	As *oi* in *oil* or as *oy* in *boy*.	*Beutel* (boi'-tĕl), pouch *Häuser* (hoi'-zĕr), houses

CONSONANTS

Most German consonants are similar to their English equivalents. Double consonants are pronounced as the corresponding single consonants. They generally indicate that the vowel preceding them is short.

The consonants *b, d, f, h, k, l, m, n, p, t* and *x* are pronounced almost as in English. *B, d* and *g* at the end of a word are usually pronounced as their voiceless counterparts *p, t* and *k*, respectively. (See exception for *-ig* ending below.) The following consonants in German are not pronounced as in English:

GERMAN SPELLING	PHONETIC SYMBOL	DESCRIPTION	EXAMPLES
ch	*kh*	Somewhat as *h* in *hue*, but much more strongly aspirated; pronounced in the back of the mouth. Occurs after *a, o, u* and *au*.	*Bach* (bakh), brook *rauchen* (rou'-khĕn), to smoke

GERMAN SPELLING	PHONETIC SYMBOL	DESCRIPTION	EXAMPLES
ch	CH	As the "kh" sound described above, but in the front of the mouth. It occurs after *ä, ai, äu, e, ei, i, ö,* and *ü* as well as after consonants. Also at the beginning of words before *e* and *i*.	*Teich* (tĭCH), pond *lächerlich* (le'-CHĕr-lĭCH), ridiculous *licht* (lĭCHt), light *solcher* (zol'-CHĕr), such *Chemie* (CHeh-mee'), chemistry *Chirurg* (CHi-roork'), surgeon
ch	sh	In words of French origin.	*Chef* (shef), chief *Champignon* (sham-pi-nyong'), mushroom
ch	k	Generally in words of Greek origin.	*Chlor* (klohr), chlorine *chronisch* (kroh'-nish), chronic
g	g	The German *g* is mostly pronounced as the *g* in *gold,* except as indicated below.	*Geld* (gelt), money *Grenze* (gren'-tsĕ), border *vergessen* (fĕr-ge'-sĕn), to forget
g	CH	In words ending in *-ig,* just as the *ch* sound described above for *Teich,* etc.	*geizig* (gī-tsiCH), stingy *siebzig* (zeep'-tsiCH), seventy
g	k	Generally at the end of a word, except when preceded by *i* (see above).	*Burg* (boork), castle *Tag* (tahk), day
g	zh	In words of French origin as *s* in *pleasure* when preceding *e* or *i*.	*girieren* (zhi-ree'rĕn), to endorse *Genie* (zhĕ-nee'), genius
j	y	As *y* in *yes*.	*Jahre* (yah'-rĕ), years
j	zh	In words of French origin as *s* in *pleasure*.	*Journalist* (zhur-nah-list'), reporter

GERMAN SPELLING	PHONETIC SYMBOL	DESCRIPTION	EXAMPLES
r	**r**	Generally uvular as in French, but in some regions, especially of Austria, it is trilled by quickly vibrating the tongue against the upper gumridge.	*braun* (broun), brown *Rinderbraten* (rin'-dĕr-brah-tĕn), roast beef
s	**z**	At the beginning of a word, and between and before vowels, as *z* in *zoom*.	*sieben* (zee'-bĕn), seven *Hosen* (hoh'-zĕn), trousers
s, ss, sz	**s**	Single *s* at the end of a word or double *s* (spelled *ss* or *sz*) always as *s* in *seek*.	*Maus* (mous), mouse *hassen* (ha'-sĕn), to hate *Mass, Masz* (mahs), measure
v	**f**	Generally as English *f*.	*von* (fon), of, by
v	**v**	Between vowels as English *v*.	*Novelle* (noh-ve'-lĕ), short story
w	**v**	Approximately as English *v*, but with the breath-stream partially impeded by pressing the lower lip against the upper teeth.	*Wasser* (va'-sĕr), water *Wurst* (voorst), sausage
z	**ts**	Always as English *ts*.	*verzeihen* (fĕr-tsī'-ĕn), to forgive

CONSONANT COMBINATIONS

GERMAN SPELLING	PHONETIC SYMBOL	DESCRIPTION	EXAMPLES
chs	**ks**	As *x* in *six*.	*sechs* (zeks), six
dt	**t**	As *t* in *city*.	*Stadt* (shtat), city *städtisch* (shte'-tish), municipal
ng	**ng**	As *ng* in *ring*.	*Wange* (vang'-ĕ), cheek

GERMAN SPELLING	PHONETIC SYMBOL	DESCRIPTION	EXAMPLES
pf	**pf**	As *pf* in *helpful*.	*Pferd* (pfehrt), horse
ps	**ps**	As *ps* in *rhapsody*.	*Psalm* (psalm), psalm
qu	**kv**	As *k* followed by German *w*.	*quer* (kvehr), across
sch	**sh**	Somewhat as *sh* in *ship*, but followed by a weak sound of the *ch* of *Teich* (see above), so that *Schiff* would be transcribed approximately as *shchif*.	*schmutzig* (shmu'-tsicн), dirty *Asche* (a'-shě), ashes *Fisch* (fish), fish
sp, st	**shp, sht**	At the beginning of a word (except in loan words) the *s* before *p* and *t* generally sounds as *sh*.	*Stuhl* (shtool), chair *spielen* (shpee'-lĕn), to play
th	**t**	Always a pure *t*, never the English *th* sound.	*Theorie* (teh-oh-ree'), theory *Thron* (trohn), throne
tz	**ts**	Always as German z, i.e. English *ts*.	*Hitze* (hi'-tsě), heat

Note. The German suffix *-tion*, corresponding to the English *-tion*, is always pronounced as *-tsiohn*: *Organisation* (or-gah-ni-za-tsiohn'), organization.

ACCENT

The main accent of the words is indicated in the phonetic transcription of the phrases with an accent mark (') *following* the syllable to be stressed.

ORTHOGRAPHY

All German nouns as well as other parts of speech functioning as nouns are written with a capital letter at the beginning.

All dependent clauses must be separated from the main clause by commas, whether or not they have a limiting meaning: *Der Herr, den Sie auf der Brücke sehen, ist der Kapitän* (The gentleman you see on the bridge is the captain).

BASIC SENTENCE PATTERNS

In each language there are a few basic types of sentences which are used more often than others in everyday speech.

On the basis of such sentences, it is possible to form many others by substituting one or two of the words of each of these basic sentences. The sentences selected to illustrate the basic patterns are short, easy to memorize and useful. Learning them before you tackle the main section of the book with the phrases which cover everyday needs and travel situations, you will acquire an idea of the structure of the language. You will also learn indirectly through these basic types of sentences some of the most important grammatical categories and their function in the construction of the sentences the natural way— the way they are encountered in actual usage.

Cross references have been supplied to establish a correlation between the basic sentence patterns and the Grammar section in this book. This will help you to relate the grammatical knowledge you'll acquire passively going through the sentences to the systematic presentation of the basic facts of grammar. For example, when you encounter the phrase "See 4.5" in the first group of sentences, it means that by turning to chapter 4, subdivision 5 in the Grammar section you will find a description of the interrogative pronouns and their uses.

BASIC QUESTIONS AND ANSWERS
(See 4.5; 4.1; 4.3; 2.0-3; 8.1)

Who is he?
He is my father (uncle, grandfather).
Wer ist das?
Das ist mein Vater (Onkel, Grossvater).
vehr ist das?
das ist mīn fah'-tĕr (ong'-kĕl, grohs'-fah-tĕr).

Who is she?
She is my mother (aunt, grandmother).
Wer ist das?
Das ist meine Mutter (Tante, Grossmutter).
vehr ist das?
das ist mī-nĕ mu'-tĕr (tan'-tĕ, grohs'-mu-tĕr).

Who is that boy?
He is my brother (cousin, nephew).
Wer ist der Junge?
Das ist mein Bruder (Vetter, Neffe).
vehr ist dehr yung'-ĕ?
das ist mīn broo'-dĕr (fe-t˘r, ne'-fĕ).

13

Who is the other boy?   *That's my older brother.*
Wer ist der andere Junge?   **Das ist mein älterer Bruder.**
vehr ist dehr an'-dĕ-rĕ yung'ĕ?   *das ist mīn el'-tĕ-rĕr broo'-dĕr.*

Who is that girl?
Wer ist dieses Mädchen?
vehr ist dee'-zĕs meht'-cнĕn?

She is my younger sister (cousin, niece).
Sie ist meine jüngere Schwester (Kusine, Nichte).
zee ist mĩ'-nĕ yü'-ngĕ-rĕ shve'-stĕr (koo-zee'-nĕ, nicн'-tĕ).

Who are they?   They are my grandparents.
Wer sind sie?   **Sie sind meine Grosseltern.**
vehr zint zee?   *zee zint mĩ'nĕ grohs'-el-tĕrn.*

This tall girl is my girl friend.   Is that so?
Dieses grosse Mädchen ist meine Freundin. (See 4.4)   **Ist das wahr?**
dee'-zĕs groh'-sĕ meht'- cнĕn ist mĩ'-nĕ froin'-din.   *ist das vahr?*

Where is my hat?   Here it is.
Wo ist mein Hut? (See 7.5)   **Hier ist er.**
voh ist mīn hoot?   *heer ist ehr.*

Where is your briefcase?   It's over there.
Wo ist Ihre Aktentasche?   **Dort ist sie.**
voh ist ee'-rĕ ak'-tĕn-ta-shĕ?   *dort ist zee.*

Where's her handbag?   It's over here.
Wo ist ihre Handtasche?   **Sie ist hier.**
voh ist ee'-rĕ hant'-tashĕ?   *zee ist heer.*

Where's the washroom?   It's on the right (left).
Wo ist die Toilette (das Badezimmer)?   **Sie (es) ist rechts (links).**
voh ist dee toa-le'-tĕ (das bah'-dĕ-tsi-mĕr)?   *zee (es) ist recнts (lingks).*

Where is John's room?   It's straight ahead.
Wo ist Johanns Zimmer?   **Es ist geradeaus.**
voh ist yo'-hans tsi'-mĕr?   *es ist gĕ-rah'-dĕ-ous.*

Where is Mary's room?   It's one flight up.
Wo ist Marias Zimmer?   **Es ist ein Stock(werk) höher.**
voh ist mah-ree'-ahs tsi'-mĕr?   *es ist īn stok(vĕrk) höh'-ĕr.*

(See 4.1-5)

Who has my notebooks? Paul has them.
Wer hat meine Notizbücher? Paul hat sie.
vehr hat mĩ-nĕ no-tits'-bü-cнĕr? poul hat zee.

With whom were you talking?
Mit wem hast du gesprochen?
mit vehm hast doo gĕ-shpro'-khĕn?

With my friend Peter.
Mit meinem Freund Peter.
mit mī'-nĕm froint peh'-tĕr.

Who are those men?
Wer sind die Männer?
vehr zint dee me'-ner?

They are my son's friends.
Sie sind die Freunde meines Sohn(e)s.
zee zint dee froin'-dĕ mī-nĕs zoh'-n(ĕs).

Who are those girls?
Wer sind die Mädchen?
vehr zint dee meht'-cHen?

They are my daughter's schoolmates.
Sie sind Mitschülerinnen (or: Schulfreundinnen) meiner Tochter.
zee zint mit'-shü-lĕr-in-nen (shul'-froin-din-nĕn) mī-nĕr tokh-tĕr.

What did she say?
Was hat sie gesagt?
vas hat zee gĕ-zahkt?

She said she couldn't come.
Sie hat gesagt, dass sie nicht kommen kann.
zee hat gĕ-zahkt', das zee nicHt ko'mĕn kan.

What is love? It's a wonderful feeling.
Was ist Liebe? Es ist ein wundervolles Gefühl.
vas ist lee'-bĕ? es ist īn vun'-dĕr-fol-ĕs ge-fühl'.

What is your occupation?
Was ist Ihr Beruf?
vas ist eer bĕ-ruf'?

I am a salesman.
Ich bin Verkäufer.
icH bin fĕr-koi'-fĕr.

Which one of these books do you like best? This one.
Welches von diesen Büchern gefällt Ihnen am besten? Dieses. (See 7.3)
vel'-cHĕs fon dee'-zĕn bü-cHĕrn gĕ-felt' ee'-nĕn am be'-stĕn? dee'-zĕs.

SENTENCES WITH *HIM, HER* AND *IT*

(*Personal Object Pronouns*)

(See 4.1, 4.1a-b; 8.2)

Henry gave it to him.
Heinz hat es ihm gegeben.
hints hat es eem gĕ-geh'-bĕn.

He gave it to me.
Er hat es mir gegeben.
ehr hat es meer gĕ-geh'-bĕn.

I gave it to her.
Ich habe es ihr gegeben.
icH hah'-bĕ es eer gĕ-geh'-bĕn.

She sent it to us.
Sie hat es uns geschickt.
zee hat es uns gĕ-shikt'.

We gave it to you.
Wir haben es Ihnen (dir; euch) gegeben. (See 4.1.a)
veer hah'-bĕn es ee'-nĕn (deer; oiᴄн) gĕ-geh'-bĕn.

You did not give it to them.
Sie haben (Du hast; Ihr habt) es ihnen nicht gegeben.
zee hah'-bĕn (doo hast; eer hapt) es ee'-nĕn niᴄнt gĕ-geh'-bĕn.

Give it to me.
Geben Sie (or: Gib, Gebt) es mir! (See 8.5)
geh'-bĕn zee (or: gip, gept) es meer!

Don't give it to him.
Geben Sie (or: Gib, Gebt) es ihm nicht!
geh'-bĕn zee (or: gip, gehpt) es eem niᴄнt!

Send it to her.
Schicken Sie es ihr! (polite singular & plural)
shi'-kĕn zee es eer.

Schicke es ihr! (familiar singular)   **Schickt es ihr!** (familiar plural)
shi'-kĕ es eer.   *shikt es eer.*

Mail it to us. Don't mail it to them.
Schicken Sie es uns! Schicken Sie es ihnen nicht!
shi'-kĕn zee es uns. shi'-kĕn zee es ee'-nĕn niᴄнt.

SENTENCES ON THE USE OF *THE, AN,* AND *A*
(*The Articles;* See 1.1-4)

Switzerland is one of the most beautiful countries in Europe.
Die Schweiz ist eines der schönsten Länder in Europa.
dee shvīts ist īnes dehr shön'-stĕn len'-dĕr in oi'-roh-pah.

Bonn is the capital of the German Federal Republic.
Bonn ist die Hauptstadt der Deutschen Bundesrepublik.
Bon' ist dee houpt'-shtat dehr doit'-shĕn bun'-dĕs-re-pub-lik.

She lives on 10th Street.
Sie wohnt in der zehnten Strasse.
zee vohnt in dehr tsehn'-tĕn shtrah'-sĕ.

The soldier carries the gun.
Der Soldat trägt das Gewehr.
dehr zol-dat' tregt das ge-vehr'.

Careful driving promotes traffic safety.
Vorsichtiges Fahren fördert die Verkehrssicherheit.
for'-ziCH-tigĕs fah'-rĕn för'-dĕrt dee fĕr-kehrs'-zi-CHĕr-hīt.

He is a dancer.	She is an intelligent girl.
Er ist Tänzer.	**Sie ist ein kluges Mädchen.**
ehr ist ten'-tsĕr.	*zee ist īn kloo'-gĕs meht'-CHĕn.*

What a fool!	What a pity!
Was für ein Narr!	**Schade!**
was für īn nar!	*shah'-dĕ!*

USE OF WORDS LIKE *ANYBODY* AND *ANYTHING*
(*The Indefinite Pronouns*)

(See 4.7)

Has anybody come? Nobody has come.
Ist jemand gekommen? Niemand ist gekommen.
ist yeh'-mant gĕ-ko'-mĕn? nee'-mant ist gĕ-ko'-mĕn.

Has anybody been here? Somebody has been here.
Ist jemand hier gewesen? Jemand ist hier gewesen.
ist yeh'-mant heer gĕ-veh'-zĕn? yeh'-mant ist heer gĕ-veh'-zĕn.

Have you received any letters? Yes, I received some.
Haben Sie Briefe erhalten? Ja, ich habe einige erhalten.
hah'-bĕn zee bree'-fĕ er-hal'-tĕn? yah, iCH hah'-bĕ ī'-nigĕ er-hal'-tĕn.

No, I have not received any.
Nein, ich habe keine erhalten.
nīn, iCH hah'-bĕ kī'-nĕ er-hal'-tĕn.

Have you got any American magazines? Yes, I have some. Here is one.
Haben Sie amerikanische Zeitschriften? Ja, ich habe einige.
   Hier ist eine.
*hah'-bĕn zee a-meh-ree-kah'-nishĕ tsīt'-shrif-tĕn? yah, iCH hah'-bĕ
ī-ni-gĕ. heer ist ī'-nĕ.*

Have you got any English newspapers? I'm sorry. I don't have any.
Haben Sie englische Zeitungen? Es tut mir leid. Ich habe keine.
*hah'-bĕn zee eng'-li-shĕ tsī'-tung-ĕn? es toot meer līt.
   iCH hah'-bĕ kī'-nĕ.*

Have you got a light? Sorry, no.
Haben Sie Feuer? Nein, leider nicht.
hah'-bĕn zee foi'-ĕr? nīn, lī'-dĕr niCHt.

Do you sell milk here? Yes, we do. Please give me a bottle.
Verkaufen Sie Milch hier? Jawohl. Bitte, geben Sie mir eine Flasche.
*fĕr-kou'-fĕn zee milcн heer? yah-vohl'. bi'-tĕ, geh'-bĕn zee meer ī'-nĕ
fla'-shĕ.*

Have you got any money? No, I have no money.
Haben Sie Geld? Nein, ich habe kein Geld.
hah'-bĕn zee gelt? nīn, icн hah'bĕ kīn gelt.

What did you eat? I ate some cheese.
Was haben Sie gegessen? Ich habe etwas Käse gegessen.
vas hah'-bĕn zee gĕ-ge'-sĕn? icн hah'-bĕ et'-vas keh'-zĕ gĕ-ge'-sĕn.

What did you buy? I bought some dresses and a suit.
**Was haben Sie gekauft? Ich habe einige Kleider und ein
        Kostüm gekauft.**
*vas hah'-bĕn zee gĕ-kouft? icн hah'bĕ ī-ni-gĕ klī-dĕr unt
        īn ko-stüm' gĕ-kouft'.*

SENTENCES ON ADJECTIVES
(See 3.1-9)

Helen is taller than Mary.
Helene ist grösser als Maria.
heh-leh'-nĕ ist grö'-sĕr als mah-ree'-ah.

Meg is less humorous than Betty.
Gretchen hat weniger Humor als Liese.
greht'-cнĕn hat veh'-ni-gĕr hu-mohr' als lee'-zĕ.

Kate is as tall as Mary.
Kätchen ist so gross wie Maria.
keht'-cнĕn ist zoh grohs vee Mah-ree'-ah.

Kate is not so tall as Mary.
Kätchen ist nicht so gross wie Maria.
keht'-cнĕn ist nicнt zoh grohs vee mah-ree'-ah.

Ann is the tallest of the girls.
Anna ist das grösste der Mädchen.
A'-na ist das grö'-stĕ dehr meht'-cнĕn.

This street has more traffic.
Diese Strasse hat mehr Verkehr.
dee'-zĕ shtrah'-sĕ hat mehr fer-kehr'.

I will take a little more meat.
Ich nehme etwas mehr Fleisch.
icн neh'-mĕ ĕt'-vas mehr flīsh.

Please have some more.
Bitte, nehmen Sie etwas mehr!
bi'-tĕ, neh'-mĕn zee ĕt'-vas mehr!

I don't want any more.
Ich will nicht mehr.
iCH vil niCHt mehr.

They don't want to stay here any longer.
Sie wollen nicht länger hier bleiben.
(or: Sie wollen nicht mehr hier bleiben.)
zee vo'-lĕn niCHt leng'-ĕr heer blī-bĕn. (or: zee vo'-lĕn niCHt mehr heer blī-bĕn.)

He can no longer go there.
Er kann nicht mehr dort hingehen.
ehr kan niCHt mehr dort hin'-geh-ĕn.

The girl with the blue silk dress was chosen queen of the ball.
Das Mädchen im blauen Seidenkleid wurde zur Ballkönigin gewählt.
das meht'-chĕn im blou'-ĕn sī-dĕn-klīt vur'-dĕ tsur bal'-kö-ni-gin gĕ-vehlt'.

My tall friend has a new red car.
Mein grosser Freund hat einen neuen roten Wagen.
mīn groh'-sĕr froint hat ī'-nĕn noi'-ĕn roh'-ten vah'-gĕn.

BASIC TYPES OF SENTENCES
(See 8.1; 6.3)

Affirmative: This lesson is easy.
Diese Lektion ist leicht.
dee'-zĕ lek-tsiohn' ist līCHt.

Negative: This lesson is not difficult.
Diese Lektion ist nicht schwer.
dee'-zĕ lek-tsiohn' ist niCHt shvehr.

Interrogative: Is this lesson easy?
Ist diese Lektion leicht?
Ist dee'-zĕ lek-tsiohn' līCHt?
It's easy.
Sie ist leicht.
zee ist līCHt.

Isn't this room large?
Ist dieses Zimmer nicht gross?
ist dee'-zĕs tsi'-mĕr niCHt grohs?
Yes, it's large.
Ja, es ist gross.
yah, es ist grohs.

(See also 8.2; 2.1-3)
I gave Claire the book.
Ich habe Klara das Buch gegeben.
iCH hah'-bĕ klah'-ra das bookh gĕ-geh'-bĕn.

I gave it to Claire.
Ich habe es Klara gegeben.
ich hah'-bĕ es klah'-ra gĕ-geh-bĕn.

I gave it to him.
Ich habe es ihm gegeben.
ich hah-bĕ es eem gĕ-geh'-bĕn.

She went there.
Sie ging hin.
zee ging hin.

Did he go there?
Ging er hin?
ging ehr hin?

He didn't go there.
Er ging nicht hin.
ehr ging nicht hin.

Didn't they go there?
Gingen sie nicht hin?
ging'-ĕn zee nicht hin?

Yes, they went there.
Ja, sie sind dort hingegangen.
yah, zee zint dort hin'-gĕ-gang'-ĕn.

I want to go to school.
Ich will in die Schule gehen.
ich vil in dee shoo'-lĕ geh'-ĕn.

You don't want to go to school.
Du willst nicht in die Schule gehen. (or: Ihr wollt . . .
doo vilst nicht in dee shoo'-lĕ geh'-ĕn (or: eer volt . . .

Who wants to go to school?
Wer will in die Schule gehen?
vehr vil in dee shoo'-lĕ geh'-ĕn?

Do they really want to go to school?
Wollen sie wirklich in die Schule gehen?
vol'-ĕn zee virk'-lich in dee shoo'-lĕ geh'-ĕn?

USES OF *WHO* AND *WHICH*; WORD ORDER
(*Relative Pronouns*; See 4.6; 6.1-4)

Who is the lady with whom I saw you last night?
Wer ist die Dame, mit der ich dich gestern gesehen habe (or: sah)?
*vehr ist dee dah'-mĕ, mit dehr ich dich ges'-tĕrn gĕ-zeh'-ĕn hah'-bĕ
    (or: zah)?*

She is my aunt who just came from Europe.
Sie ist meine Tante, die gerade von Europa ankam.
        (or: angekommen ist.)
*zee ist mĭ'-nĕ tan'-tĕ, dee gĕ-rah'-dĕ fon oi-roh'-pah an'-kahm.
        (or: an'-gĕ-ko-mĕn ist.)*

Those who study languages with records can pronounce them correctly
and learn them more easily.

**Wer Sprachen mit Schallplatten studiert, kann sie richtig
aussprechen und leichter erlernen.**

vehr shprah'-khĕn mit shal'-pla-tĕn shtoo-deert', kan zee rich*'-tich
ous'-shpre-*chĕn *und* lich*'-tĕr er-ler'-nĕn.*

The girl to whom I was speaking is my fiancee.

Das Mädchen, zu dem ich sprach, ist meine Verlobte (or: Braut).

das met'-chĕn, tsoo dehm ich *shprahkh ist mĭ'-nĕ fĕr-lohp-tĕ
(or: brout).*

The boy whose father is my teacher lives here.

Der Junge (Knabe), dessen Vater mein Lehrer ist, wohnt hier.

dehr yung'-ĕ (knah'-bĕ), de'-sĕn fah'-tĕr mīn leh'-rĕr ist, vohnt heer.

Don't tell me that this blue book is not yours.

Sag mir nicht, dass dieses blaue Buch nicht deins ist.

zag meer nicht*, das dee'-zĕs blou'-ĕ bookh* nicht *dīns ist.*

When she came, he left.

Als sie kam, ging er.

als zee kahm, ging ehr.

If Kurt comes, I will tell him about it.

**Wenn Kurt kommt, erzähl ich es ihm. (or: Wenn Kurt kommt,
werde ich es ihm sagen.)**

ven kurt komt, er-tsel ich *es eem (or: ven kurt komt, vehr'-dĕ* ich
es eem zah'-gĕn).

If Kurt came, I would tell him about it.

Sollte Kurt kommen, so würde ich mit ihm darüber sprechen.

zol'-tĕ kurt ko'-mĕn, zoh vür'-dĕ ich *mit eem dah-rü'-bĕr shpre-*chen*.*

If Kurt had come, I would have told him about it.

Wenn Kurt gekommen wäre, so hätte ich mit ihm darüber gesprochen.

ven kurt gĕ-ko'-mĕn veh'-rĕ, zoh he'-tĕ ich *mit eem dah-rü'-bĕr
gĕ-shpro'-khĕn.*

When Kurt arrived (came), I told him the news.

Als Kurt ankam (kam), erzählte ich ihm die Neuigkeit(en).

*als kurt an-kahm (kahm), er-tsel'-tĕ ich eem dee noi'-*ich*-kit(ĕn).*

If Kurt had not come, I would have been very angry (with him).

**Wenn Kurt nicht gekommen wäre, so wäre ich (ihm)
sehr böse gewesen.**

ven kurt nicht *ge-ko'-mĕn veh'-rĕ, zoh veh'-rĕ* ich *eem zehr böh-zĕ
gĕ-veh'-zĕn.*

EVERYDAY CONVERSATIONS

BASIC EXPRESSIONS

Good morning.
Guten Morgen!
goo'-těn mor'-gěn!

Good evening.
Guten Abend!
goo'-těn ah'-běnt!

Good night.
Gute Nacht!
goo'-tě nakht!

Goodbye.
Auf Wiedersehen!
ouf vee'-děr-zehn!

Hello.
Hallo! (Guten Tag!)
ha'loh! (goo'-těn tahk!)

Thank you.
Danke!
dang'-kě!

You're welcome.
Bitte!
bit'-ě!

Excuse me.
Entschuldigen Sie!
ent-shul'-dee-gěn zee!

Please.
Bitte!
bi'-tě!

How much is it?
Wieviel kostet es?
vee-feel' kos'-tět es?

Where?
Wo?
voh?

When?
Wann?
van?

I want.
Ich will.
iCH vil.

Give me.
Geben Sie mir!
geh'-běn zee meer!

Gib mir!
gip meer!

Gebt mir!
gehpt meer!

Where is (are) . . .?
Wo ist (sind) . . .?
voh ist (zint) . . .?

Do you speak English?
Sprechen Sie englisch?
shpre'-CHěn zee eng'-lish?

I don't understand.
Ich verstehe nicht.
iCH fer-shteh'-ě niCHt.

Speak more slowly.
Sprechen Sie (or: Sprich, Sprecht) langsamer!
shpre'-CHen zee (or: shpriCH, shpreCHt) lang'-zah-mer!

My name is Heidi.
Ich heisse Heidi.
iCH hī'-sě hī'-di.

How do you do?
Wie geht es Ihnen (or: dir, euch)?
vee geht es eenen (or: deer, oiCH)?

22

GETTING TO KNOW YOU

May I present Mr. (Mrs., Miss) Newman?
Darf ich Herrn (Frau, Fräulein) Neumann vorstellen?
darf iCH hern (frou, froi'-lĭn) noi'-man fohr'-shte-lĕn?

This is my wife.
Das ist meine Frau.
das ist mī'-nĕ frou.

And this is my son (daughter).
Und das ist mein Sohn (meine Tochter).
unt das ist mīn zohn (mī'-nĕ tokh'-tĕr).

You speak German, I see.
Sie sprechen deutsch, wie ich sehe.
zee shpre'-CHĕn doitsh, vee iCH zeh'-ĕ.

A little, but quite poorly.
Ein wenig, aber sehr schlecht.
īn veh'-niCH, ah'-bĕr zehr shleCHt.

Not at all. Can you understand what I'm saying?
Keineswegs (or: Durchaus nicht). Können Sie verstehen, was ich sage?
kī-nes-veks (durCH-ous' niCHt). kö-nĕn zee fer'-shteh-ĕn, vas iCH zah'-gĕ?

Is this your first trip to Germany?
Sind Sie jetzt zum ersten Mal in Deutschland?
zint zee yetst tsum ehr'-stĕn mahl in doitsh'-lant?

Yes, my first trip.
Ja, meine erste Reise.
yah, mī'-nĕ ehr'-stĕ rī'-zĕ.

Are you enjoying yourself?
Unterhalten Sie sich gut?
un-tĕr-hal'-tĕn zee siCH goot?

Very much. I like the country.
Sehr! Das Land gefällt mir.
zehr! das lant gĕ-felt' meer.

Where do you live in the United States?
Wo wohnen Sie in den Vereinigten Staaten?
voh voh'-nĕn zee in dehn fĕr-ī-nik-tĕn shtah'-tĕn?

I live in New York.
Ich wohne in New York.
iCH voh'-nĕ in New York.

If you ever come my way, look me up (*lit.:* visit me).
Besuchen Sie mich, wenn Sie jemals in meine Gegend kommen.
bĕ-zoo'-khĕn zee miCH, ven zee yeh'-mahls in mī'-nĕ geh'-gent ko'-mĕn.

Very kind of you. I hope I shall be able to accept.
Das ist sehr freundlich von Ihnen. Ich hoffe, dass ich annehmen kann.
das ist zehr froint'-liCH fon ee'-nĕn. iCH ho'-fĕ, das iCH an'-neh-mĕn kan.

Perhaps we can have lunch.
Vielleicht können wir zu Mittag essen.
vee-lĩcht kö-nĕn veer tsoo mi'-tahk e'-sĕn.

Or drink an apéritif before you leave.
Oder trinken wir noch ein Gläschen, bevor Sie abfahren.
oh'-dĕr tring'-kĕn veer nokh in gleh'-shĕn, bĕ-fohr zee ap'-fahrĕn.

I have a letter of introduction for Mr. Miller.
Ich habe einen Empfehlungsbrief an Herrn Müller.
iCH hah'-be ĩ-nĕn ĕm-pfeh'-lungs-breef an hern mü'-lĕr.

I will be in Berlin for ten days.
Ich werde mich zehn Tage in Berlin aufhalten.
iCH vehr'-dĕ miCH tsehn tah'-gĕ in ber-leen' ouf'-hal-tĕn.

COUNTING

The Cardinal Numbers

one	six	eleven	sixteen
eins	**sechs**	**elf**	**sechzehn**
ĩns	*zeks*	*elf*	*zeCH'-tsehn*
two	seven	twelve	seventeen
zwei	**sieben**	**zwölf**	**siebzehn**
tsvĩ	*zee'-bĕn*	*tsvölf*	*zeep'-tsehn*
three	eight	thirteen	eighteen
drei	**acht**	**dreizehn**	**achtzehn**
drĩ	*akht*	*drĩ'-tsehn*	*akh'-tsehn*
four	nine	fourteen	nineteen
vier	**neun**	**vierzehn**	**neunzehn**
feer	*noin*	*feer'-tsehn*	*noin'-tsehn*
five	ten	fifteen	twenty
fünf	**zehn**	**fünfzehn**	**zwanzig**
fünf	*tsehn*	*fünf'-tsehn*	*tsvan'-tsiCH*

twenty-one **einundzwanzig** *īn'-unt- . . .*	fifty **fünfzig** *fünf'-tsiCH*	ninety **neunzig** *noin'-tsiCH*
twenty-two **zweiundzwanzig** *tsvī-unt- . . .*	sixty **sechzig** *zeCH'-tsiCH*	ninety-one **einundneunzig** *īn'-unt- . . .*
thirty **dreissig** *drī'-siCH*	seventy **siebzig** *zeep'-tsiCH*	one hundred **hundert** *hun'-dĕrt*
thirty-one **einunddreissig** *īn'-unt- . . .*	seventy-one **einundsiebzig** *īn'-unt- . . .*	one thousand **tausend** *tou'-zĕnt*
forty **vierzig** *feer'-tsiCH*	eighty **achtzig** *akh-tsiCH*	one million **eine Million** *ī'-ne mil-iohn'*
forty-one **einundvierzig** *īn'-unt- . . .*	eighty-one **einundachtzig** *īn'-unt- . . .*	

The Ordinal Numbers

first **erste** *ehr'-stĕ*	fourth **vierte** *feer'-tĕ*	seventh **siebente** *zee'-bĕn-tĕ*	tenth **zehnte** *tsehn'-tĕ*
second **zweite** *tsvī'-tĕ*	fifth **fünfte** *fünf'-tĕ*	eighth **achte** *akh'-tĕ*	eleventh **elfte** *elf'-tĕ*
third **dritte** *drī'-tĕ*	sixth **sechste** *zek'-stĕ*	ninth **neunte** *noin'-tĕ*	twelfth **zwölfte** *tsvölf'-tĕ*

The Fractions

half **halb; die Hälfte** *halp; dee helf'-tĕ*	one fourth **ein Viertel** *īn feer'-tĕl*	one eighth **ein Achtel** *īn akh'-tel*
a third **ein Drittel** *īn dri'-tĕl*	three quarters **drei Viertel** *drī feer'-tĕl*	one and a half **anderthalb** *an'-dĕrt-halp*

THE CLOCK AND THE CALENDAR

What time is it?
Wieviel Uhr ist es? (Wie spät ist es?)
vee-feel' oor ist es? (vee shpeht ist es?)

It is ten a.m.
Es ist zehn Uhr vormittags.
es ist tsehn oor fohr'-mi-tahks.

It is a quarter past three p.m.
Es ist ein Viertel nach drei nachmittags (or: viertel vier).
es ist īn feer'-tĕl nahkh drī nahkh'-mi-tahks (or: feer'-tĕl feer)

(or: **Es ist drei Uhr fünfzehn.**)
(or *est drī oor fünf'-tsehn.*)

It is half past six.
Es ist halb sieben.
ist halp zee'-bĕn.

It is quarter to nine.
Es ist (ein) Viertel vor neun.
es ist (īn) feer'-tĕl fohr noin.

The days of the week are: Monday, Tuesday, Wednesday, Thursday,
     Friday, Saturday, Sunday.
**Die Tage der Woche sind: Montag, Dienstag, Mittwoch, Donnerstag,
     Freitag, Samstag (or: Sonnabend), Sonntag.**
*dee tah'-gĕ dehr vo'-khĕ zint: mohn'-tahk, deens'-tahk, mit'-vokh,
     do'-nĕrs-tahk, frītahk, zams'-tahk (or zon'-ah-bĕnt), zon'-tahk.*

The months of the year are: January, February, March, April, May,
     June, July, August, September, October, November, December.
**Die Monate des Jahres sind: Januar, Februar, März, April, Mai, Juni,
     Juli, August, September, Oktober, November, Dezember.**
*dee moh'-na-tĕ des yah'-res zind: ya'noo-ar, feh'-broo-ar, merts, a-pril',
     mī, yoo'-ni, yoo'-li, ou-gust, zep-tem'-bĕr, ok-toh'-bĕr,
     noh-vem'-bĕr, deh-tsem'-bĕr.*

The seasons of the year are: Spring, Summer, Autumn, Winter.
Die Jahreszeiten sind: Frühling, Sommer, Herbst, Winter.
dee yah'rĕs-tsī-tĕn zint: früh'-ling, zo'-mer, herpst, vin'-tĕr.

How is the weather?
Wie ist das Wetter?
vee ist das ve'-tĕr?

It is a beautiful day.
Es ist ein schöner Tag.
es ist īn shöh'-nĕr tahk.

It is fine.
Es ist schön.
es ist shöhn.

It is raining (snowing).
Es regnet (schneit).
es rehg'-nĕt (shnīt).

It is drizzling.
Es regnet leicht.
es rehg'-nĕt līcHt.

What are the holidays in Germany?
Was für (Welche) Feiertage gibt es in Deutschland?
vas führ (vel'-CHĕ) fī'-ĕr-tah-gĕ gipt es in doitsh'-lant?

New Year's Day, Easter, Whitsuntide (Pentecost), Christmas.
Neujahr, Ostern, Pfingsten, Weihnachten.
noi'-yahr, ohs'-tĕrn, pfings'-tĕn, vī-nakh-tĕn.

I will be 31 years old on June 16, 1967.
Am sechzehnten Juni, 1967, werde ich einunddreissig Jahre alt sein.
am zech-tsehn-tĕn yoo'-ni, noin'-tsehn-hun'-dĕrt-zee'-bĕn-unt-zech'-tsich vehr-dĕ ich īn-unt-drī'-sich yah'-rĕ alt zīn.

STRANGER IN TOWN

Does anyone here speak English?
Spricht hier jemand englisch?
shpricht heer yeh'-mant eng'-lish?

I've lost my way.
Ich habe mich verlaufen.
ich hah'-bĕ mich fĕr-lou'-fĕn.

Where do you want to go?
Wo wollen Sie hin? (or: Wohin wollen Sie?)
voh vo'-lĕn zee hin? (or: voh-hin' vo'-lĕn zee?)

Do you understand me?
Verstehen Sie mich?
fĕr-shteh'-ĕn zee mich?

No, I don't understand (you).
Nein, ich verstehe (Sie) nicht.
nīn, ich fĕr-shteh'-ĕ (zee) nicht.

Please speak slowly.
Bitte, sprechen Sie langsam.
bi'-tĕ, shpre'-chen zee lang'-zahm.

I am an American.
Ich bin Amerikaner.
ich bin a-meh-ree-kah'-nĕr.

Please repeat.
Bitte, wiederholen Sie das noch einmal.
bi'-tĕ wee-dĕr-hoh-lĕn zee das nokh īn'-mahl.

What are you saying?
Was sagen Sie?
vas zah'-gĕn zee?

I can't find my wallet.
Ich kann meine Brieftasche nicht finden.
ich kan mī'-nĕ breef'-ta-shĕ nicht fin'-dĕn.

I've been robbed!
Man hat mich bestohlen.
man hat mich bĕ-shtoh'-lĕn.

(Please) call the police!
Rufen Sie die Polizei (,bitte)!
roo'-fĕn zee dee poh-lee-zī (, bi'-tĕ)!

Where is the Police Station?
Wo ist das Polizeirevier?
voh ist das poh-lee-tsī'-rĕ-veer?

That way. Help! Fire!
Dort. Hilfe! Feuer!
dort. hil'-fĕ! foi'-ĕr!

Take me to the American consul.
Führen Sie mich zum amerikanischen Konsul!
füh'-rĕn zee miCH tsum a-meh-ree-kah'-ni-shĕn kon'-zul!

I've left my overcoat on the train.
Ich habe meinen Mantel im Zug iiegen lassen.
iCH hah'-bĕ mī-nĕn man'-tel im tsook lee'-gĕn la'-sĕn.

How can I get it back?
Wie kann ich ihn zurück bekommen?
vee kan iCH ihn tsoo-rük' bĕ-ko'-men?

I cannot find my hotel.
Ich kann mein Hotel nicht finden.
iCH kan mīn hoh-tĕl' niCHt fin'-dĕn.

Can you help me?
Können Sie mir helfen?
kö'-nĕn zee meer hel'-fĕn?

I've lost my umbrella.
Ich habe meinen Regenschirm verloren.
iCH hah'-bĕ mï-nĕn reh'-gĕn-shirm fĕr-loh'-rĕn.

Can you tell me where the lost and found desk is?
Können Sie mir sagen, wo das Fundbüro ist?
kö'-nĕn zee meer zah'-gĕn, voh das funt'-bü-roh ist?

Please don't bother (annoy) me. I will call a policeman.
**Bitte, belästigen (stören) Sie mich nicht. Ich rufe einen Polizisten
        (or: Schutzmann).**
*bi'-tĕ, bĕ-le'-sti-gĕn (shtöh'-rĕn) zee miCH niCHt. iCH roo'-fĕ ï'-nĕn
        poh-lee-tsi'-stĕn (or: shuts'-man).*

Where are you taking me?
Wohin führen Sie mich?
voh-in' füh'-rĕn zee miCH?

To the police station. You are arrested.
Zum Polizeirevier (or: Zur Polizeistation). Sie sind verhaftet.
*tsum poh-lee-tsī'-rĕ-veer (or: tsur poh-lee-tsī'-shta-tsiohn).
        zee zint fĕr-haf'-tĕt.*

I need a lawyer.
Ich brauche einen Rechtsanwalt.
ich brou'-khĕ ï'-nĕn reCHts-an-valt.

Are you hurt?
Sind Sie verletzt?
zint zee fĕr-letst'?

I would like to make a (telephone) call.
Ich möchte einen Anruf machen (or: telefonieren).
iCH möCH'-tĕ ï'-nĕn an'-ruf ma'-khĕn (or: teh-lĕ-foh-nee'-rĕn).

Please let me have your name and address.
Bitte, geben Sie mir Ihren Namen und Ihre Adresse.
bi'-tě, geh-bĕn zee meer ee'-rĕn nah'-mĕn unt ee'-rĕ a-dre'-sĕ.

Let me see your driver's license.
Zeigen Sie mir Ihren Führerschein!
tsi-gĕn zee meer ee'-rĕn füh'-rĕr-shin!

What is the name of your insurance company?
Wie heisst Ihre Versicherungsgesellschaft?
vee hīst ee'-rĕ fĕr-zi'-CHĕr-ungs-gĕ-zel-shaft?

How badly damaged is your car?
Wie schwer ist Ihr Wagen beschädigt?
vee shvehr ist eer vah'-gĕn bĕ-she'-diCHt?

I have lost a suitcase.
Ich habe meinen Handkoffer verloren.
iCH hah-bĕ mī-nĕn hant'-ko-fĕr fer-loh'-rĕn.

It carries the initials A. R.
Er ist mit den Anfangsbuchstaben A. R. bezeichnet.
ehr ist mit dehn an'-fangs-bookh-shtah-bĕn ah er bĕ-tsīCH'-nĕt.

Have you a piece answering that description?
Haben Sie ein solches Gepäckstück?
hah'-bĕn zee īn zol'-CHes gĕ-pek'-shtük?

If it comes in, telephone me at Mr. Miller's.
Sollte es eintreffen, rufen Sie mich bei Herrn Müller an,
zol'-tĕ es īn'-tre-fĕn, roo-fĕn zee miCH bī hern mü'-lĕr an.

ABOARD SHIP

I am traveling cabin class. Stateroom No. 50.
Ich reise Kajüte. Kabinennummer fünfzig.
iCH rī'-zĕ ka-yü'-tĕ. ka-bee'-nĕn-nu-mĕr fünf'-tsiCH.

Can you please direct me?
Können Sie mir bitte die Richtung geben?
kö'-nĕn zee meer bi'-tĕ dee riCH-tung geh'-bĕn?

You are on C deck.
Sie sind auf dem C-Deck.
zee zint ouf dehm tseh'-dek.

Take our bags to our cabin.
Bringen Sie unser Gepäck in unsere Kajüte (Kabine).
bring'-ĕn zee un'-zĕr gĕ-pek' in un'-zĕrĕ ka-yü'-tĕ (ka-bee'-nĕ).

What time is lunch served?
Wann (or: Um wieviel Uhr) wird das Mittagessen serviert?
van (or: um vee'-feel oor) virt das mi'-tahk-e-sĕn zer-veert'?

The first sitting is at twelve.
Die erste Mahlzeit ist um zwölf Uhr.
dee ehr'-stĕ mahl'-tsīt ist um tsvölf oor.

The second at one.
Die zweite ist um eins.
dee tsvī'-tĕ ist um īns.

I would like to rent a deck chair.
Ich möchte einen Liegestuhl mieten.
iсн мöсн'-tĕ ī'-nĕn lee'-gĕ-shtool mee'-tĕn.

How much does a deck chair cost?
Wieviel kostet ein Liegestuhl?
vee'-feel ko'-stĕt īn lee'-gĕ-shtool?

The cost is three dollars.
Der Preis ist drei Dollar.
dehr prīs ist drī do-lahr'.

At what time does the boat dock tomorrow?
Um wieviel Uhr (Wann) wird das Schiff morgen anlegen?
um vee'-feel oor (van) virt das shif mor'-gĕn an'-leh-gĕn?

We will dock at Hamburg at 8:00.
Wir werden um acht Uhr in Hamburg anlegen.
veer vehr-dĕn um akht oor in ham'-boork an'-leh-gĕn.

See that my bags are off in time.
**Achten Sie darauf, dass mein Gepäck zeitig (bei Zeiten) an Land
        gebracht wird.**
*akh-tĕn zee dahr'-ouf, das mīn gĕ-pek' tsī'-tiсн
        (bī tsī-tĕn) an lant gĕ-brakht virt.*

PLANE TRAVEL

Is there a plane for Munich?
Gibt es ein Flugzeug nach München?
gibt es īn flook'-tsoik nahkh mün'-снĕn?

When does it leave?
Wann fliegt es ab?
van fleecht es ap?

How long is the flight?
Wie lange dauert der Flug?
vee langĕ dou'-ĕrt dehr flook?

What is the fare?
Was kostet die Fahrt?
vas ko'-stĕt dee fahrt?

A ticket to Cologne please.
Bitte, eine Fahrkarte nach Köln.
bi'-tĕ, ī'nĕ fahr'-kar-tĕ nahkh köln.

A seat next to the window, please.
Bitte, einen Sitzplatz am Fenster (or: einen Fensterplatz).
bi'-tĕ, ī'-nĕn zits'-plats am fen'-stĕr (or: ī-nĕn fen'-stĕr-plats).

Is lunch (dinner) served on this flight?
Wird auf diesem Flug Mittagessen (Abendessen) serviert?
virt ouf dee'-zĕm flook mi'-tahk-e-sĕn (ah'-bĕnt-e-sĕn) zer-veert'?

How much does my baggage weigh?
Wieviel wiegt mein Gepäck?
vee-feel' veekt min gĕ-pek'?

You are five pounds overweight.
Es hat fünf Pfund Übergewicht.
es hat fünf pfunt ü-bĕr'-gĕ-vicHt.

How do I get to the airport?
Wie komme ich zum Flughafen?
vee ko'-mĕ icH tsum flook'-hah-fĕn?

When does the bus leave for the airport?
Wann geht der Autobus zum Flughafen?
Van geht dehr ou'-toh-bus tsum flook'-hah-fĕn?

May I see your ticket?
Darf ich Ihre Fahrkarte sehen?
darf icH ee'-rĕ fahr'-kar-tĕ zeh'-ĕn?

You have seat number 30.
Sie haben Sitznummer dreissig.
zee hah'-bĕn zits'-nu-mĕr drï'-sicH.

Stewardess, will the plane land on schedule?
Stewardess, wird das Flugzeug fahrplanmässig landen?
Stewardess, virt das flook'-tsoik fahr-plahn-me-sicH lan'-dĕn?

Stewardess, I feel airsick.
Stewardess, ich bin luftkrank.
Stewardess, icH bin luft'-krank.

Do you have a remedy?
Haben Sie ein Heilmittel?
hah'-bĕn zee în hïl'-mi-tel?

Will the plane arrive on time?
Wird das Flugzeug pünktlich ankommen?
virt das flook'-tsoik pünkt'-licH an'-ko-mĕn?

We are scheduled to arrive in Bonn in one hour.
Wir sollen fahrplanmässig in einer Stunde in Bonn ankommen.
veer zo-lĕn fahr-plahn-me-sicH in ï'-nĕr shtun'-dĕ in bon an'-komĕn.

ALL ABOARD (TRAVEL BY RAIL)

Where is the ticket office?
Wo ist der Schalter?
voh ist dehr shal'-tĕr?

One ticket to Frankfurt.
Eine Fahrkarte nach Frankfurt.
ï'-nĕ fahr'-kar-tĕ nahhk frank'-furt.

First (Second) class.
Erste (Zweite) Klasse.
ehr'-ste (tsvï'-tĕ) kla'-sĕ.

How much is the ticket?
Wieviel kostet die Fahrkarte?
vee-feel' ko'-stĕt dee fahr'-kar-tĕ?

One way ticket.
Eine einfache Fahrkarte.
ī'-nĕ īn'-fa-khĕ fahr'-kar-tĕ.

Round trip ticket.
Hin- und Rückfahrkarte.
hin-unt rük'- fahr-kar-tĕ.

What time does this train leave?
Wann fährt dieser Zug ab?
van fert dee'-zĕr tsook ap?

When does it arrive?
Wann kommt er an?
van komt ehr an?

Is it express or a local?
Ist es ein Schnellzug (or: D-Zug) oder ein Personenzug?
ist es īn shnel'-tsook (or: deh'-tsook) oh'-dĕr īn per-zoh'-nĕn-tsook?

Is this seat taken?
Ist dieser Platz besetzt?
ist dee'-zĕr plats bĕ-zetst'?

Is smoking permitted here?
Ist Rauchen hier erlaubt?
ist rou'-khĕn heer er-loupt'?

Tickets, please.
Die Fahrkarten, bitte!
dee fahr'-kartĕn, bi'-tĕ!

The dining car is now open.
Der Speisewagen ist jetzt offen.
dehr shpī'-zĕ-vah-gĕn ist yetst o'-fĕn.

Which way is the rest room, please?
Bitte, wo ist die Toilette?
bi'-tĕ, voh ist dee toa-le'-tĕ?

Is the train on time?
Ist der Zug pünktlich?
ist dehr tsook pünkt'-liсн?

Yes, we arrive in ten minutes.
Ja, wir kommen in zehn Minuten an.
yah, veer ko'-mĕn in tsehn mee-noo'-tĕn an.

GOING THROUGH CUSTOMS

Open your baggage, please.
Bitte öffnen Sie Ihr Gepäck.
bi'-tĕ öf'-nĕn zee eer gĕ-pek'.

Do you have anything besides wearing apparel?
Haben Sie irgend etwas ausser Kleidungsstücken?
hah'-bĕn zee ir'-gent et'-vas ou'-sĕr klī'-dung-shtü-kĕn?

Yes, a few toilet articles.
Ja, einige Toilettenartikel.
yah, ī'-ni-gĕ toa-le'-tĕn-ar-ti-kĕl.

And my camera.
Und meinen (Photo)apparat.
unt mī-nĕn (fo'-toh)-a-pa-raht.

Is the camera for personal use?
Ist der (Photo)apparat für Ihren persönlichen Gebrauch?
ist dehr (fo'-toh)-a-pa-raht für ee'-rĕn per-zöhn'-li-снĕn gĕ-broukh?

Yes, it is.   How many cigarettes do you have?
Jawohl.   **Wieviel Zigaretten haben sie bei sich?**
yah-vohl'.   *vee-feel' tsee-ga-re'-tĕn hah'-bĕn zee bī zicн?*

I have two cartons (400 cigarettes).
Ich habe zwei Kartons (vier hundert Zigaretten).
icн hah'-bĕ tsvī kar-tong's (feer hun'-dĕrt tsee-ga-re'-tĕn).

That's the maximum allowed.
Das ist das erlaubte Maximum.
das ist das er-loup'-tĕ mak'-si-mum.

May I see your papers.
Zeigen Sie mir Ihre Ausweispapiere?
tzī'-gĕn zee meer ee'-rĕ ous'-vīs-pa-pee-rĕ?

Will you please get a porter?
Wollen Sie bitte einen Gepäckträger holen?
vo'-len zee bi'-tĕ ī'-nĕn gĕ-pek'-tre-gĕr hoh'-lĕn?

Porter, please take my bags.
Gepäckträger, bitte nehmen Sie meine Koffer.
gĕ-pek'-tre-gĕr, bi'-tĕ neh'-mĕn zee mī'-nĕ ko'-fer.

To the taxi stand.   To the bus station.
Zur Taxi-Haltestelle.   **Zur Autobus-Haltestelle.**
tsur tak'-see-hal'-tĕ-shte-lĕ.   *tsur ou'-toh-bus-hal'-tĕ-shte-lĕ.*

How much do you charge?   Follow me please.
Wieviel verlangen Sie?   **Bitte, folgen Sie mir.**
vee-feel' fer-lang'-ĕn zee?   *bi'-tĕ, fol'-gĕn zee meer.*

TAXI!

Taxi!   Take me to the shopping center.
Taxi!   **Bringen Sie mich zum Geschäftszentrum.**
tak'-si!   *bring'-ĕn zee micн tsum gĕ-shefts'-tsen-trum.*

I'm in a hurry.   Is there a faster way to get there?
Ich habe es eilig.   **Gibt es einen schnelleren Weg?**
icн hah'-bĕ es ī'-licн. *gipt es ī'-nĕn shne'-lĕ-rĕn vehk?*

What's this building on the right (on the left)?
Was für ein Gebäude ist das rechts (links)?
vas führ in gĕ-boi'-dĕ ist das reснts (lingks)?

Please don't drive so fast.
Bitte, fahren Sie nicht so schnell.
bi'-tĕ, fah'-rĕn zee niснt zoh shnel.

Stop at the corner.
Halten Sie an der Ecke!
hal'-tĕn zee an dehr e'-kĕ.

What's the charge?
Was kostet die Fahrt?
vas ko'-stĕt dee fahrt?

BUS STOP

Where is the bus stop?
Wo ist die Autobus-Haltestelle (or: Wo hält der Autobus)?
voh ist dee ou'-toh-bus-hal'-tĕ-shte-lĕ (or: voh helt dehr ou'-toh-bus)?

Does the bus to Cologne stop here?
Hält hier der Autobus nach Köln?
helt heer dehr ou'-toh-bus nahkh köln?

When is the next bus to Munich?
Wann fährt der nächste Autobus nach München?
van fehrt dehr nehkh'-stĕ ou'-toh-bus nahkh mün'-снĕn?

I am going to Hamburg.
Ich fahre nach Hamburg.
iсн fah'-rĕ nahkh ham'-burg.

How often do the buses run?
Wie oft fahren die Autobusse?
vee oft fah'-rĕn dee ou'-toh-bu-sĕ?

One ticket, please.
Eine Fahrkarte, bitte.
ī'-ne fahr'-kar-tĕ, bi'-tĕ.

Please let me know when we reach Bonn.
Bitte, sagen Sie es mir, wenn wir in Bonn ankommen.
bi'-tĕ, zah'-gĕn zee es meer, ven veer in bon an'-ko-mĕn.

Driver, please let me off.
Fahrer, bitte lassen Sie mich aussteigen.
fah'-rĕr, bi'-tĕ la'-sĕn zee miсн ous'-shtī-gĕn.

How late do the buses run on this line?
Wie spät fahren die Autobusse auf dieser Strecke?
vee shpeht fah'-rĕn dee ou'-toh-bu-sĕ ouf dee'-zĕr shtre'-kĕ?

MOTORING THROUGH THE COUNTRY

Where is the nearest gas station?
Wo ist die nächste Tankstelle?
voh ist dee nehkh'-stě tangk'-shte-lě?

Fill 'er up. (Fill the tank.)
Füllen Sie den Tank.
fü'-lěn zee dehn tank.

Give me 20 liters of gas.
Geben Sie mir zwanzig Liter Benzin.
geh'-běn zee meer tsvan'-tsiсн li'-těr ben-tseen'.

A liter of oil.
Ein Liter Öl.
in li'-těr öhl.

Check the oil, water and battery.
Sehen Sie nach Öl, Wasser und Batterie.
zeh'-en zee nakh öhl, va'-sěr unt ba-tˇ-ree'.

Is this the way to Wiesbaden?
Ist das der Weg nach Wiesbaden?
ist das dehr vek nahkh vis'-bah-děn?

Straight ahead 45 kilometers.
Gerade aus fünfundvierzig Kilometer.
gě-rah'-dě ous fünf-unt-feer'-tsiсн ki'-loh-meh-těr.

Please check my tires.
Bitte, prüfen Sie meine Reifen.
bi'-tě, prüh'-fěn zee mǐ'-ně rǐ'-fěn.

Turn left (right) at the next crossroad.
Biegen Sie an der nächsten Strassenkreuzung links (rechts) ab.
bee'-gěn zee an dehr nehkh'-stěn shtrah'-sěn-kroi-tsung lingks (reснts) ap.

There is a detour 18 kilometers from here.
Achtzehn Kilometer von hier ist eine Umleitung.
akht'-tsehn ki'-loh-meh-těr fon heer ist ǐ'-ně um'-lǐ-tung.

Can we reach Vienna before night fall?
Können wir Wien noch vor Dunkelheit erreichen?
kö'-něn veer veen nokh fohr dung'-kěl-hit ěr-rǐ'-снěn?

What town is this?
Welcher Ort ist das?
vel'-снěr ort ist das?

Where does this road go?
Wohin führt diese Strasse?
vo-hin' führt dee'-zě shtrah'-sě?

I have a flat tire.
Ich habe eine Panne.
iсн hah'-bě ǐ'-ně pan'-ně.

My headlights don't work.
Meine Scheinwerfer funktionieren nicht.
mǐ'-ně shin'-ver-fěr funk-tsio-nee'-rěn niснt.

Where can I have repairs done?
Wo kann ich etwas reparieren lassen?
voh kan iCH ĕt'-vas re-pa-ree'-rĕn la'-sĕn?

Send someone to repair my car.
Senden Sie jemand, um meinen Wagen zu reparieren.
zĕn'-dĕn zee yeh'-mant, um mī'-nĕn vah'-gĕn tsoo re-pa-ree'-rĕn.

May I have some water for my car, please.
Kann ich bitte etwas Wasser für meinen Wagen haben?
kan iCH bi'-tĕ ĕt'-vas va'-sĕr führ mī'-nĕn vah'-gĕn hah'-bĕn?

Please take me to the nearest garage.
Bitte, bringen Sie mich zur nächsten Garage.
bi'-tĕ, bring'-ĕn zee miCH tsoor nehkh'-stĕn ga-rah'-zhĕ.

Can you give my car a push?
Können Sie, bitte, meinen Wagen etwas anschieben?
kö'-nĕn zee, bi'-tĕ, mī'-nĕn vah'-gĕn ĕt'-vas an'-shee-bĕn?

Can you give me a lift to Salzburg?
Können Sie mich nach Salzburg mitnehmen?
kö'-nĕn zee miCH nakh zalts'-boork mit'-neh-mĕn?

AUTO CARE

Parts and Tools of the Car

Accelerator.
der Gashebel.
gahs'-heh-bĕl.

Battery.
die Batterie.
bah'-tĕ-ree.

Bumper
die Stoszstange.
shtohs'-shtang-ĕ

Brake.
die Bremse.
brem'-zĕ.

Cable.
das Kabel.
kah'-bĕl.

Chains.
die Ketten.
ke'-tĕn.

Clutch.
die Kupplung.
koo'-plung.

Door handle.
der Türgriff.
tür'-grif.

Engine.
der Motor.
mo'-tor.

Fender.
der Kotflügel.
koht'-flü-gĕl.

Hammer.
der Hammer.
ha'-mĕr.

Headlight.
der Scheinwerfer.
shin'-vehr-fĕr.

Hood.
die Haube.
hou'-bĕ.

Horn.
die Hupe.
hoo'-pĕ.

Ignition key.
der Zündschlüssel.
tsünt'-shlü-sĕl.

Jack.
der Wagenheber.
vah'-gĕn-heh-bĕr.

Key.
der Schlüssel.
shlü'-sĕl.

Pliers.
die Zange.
tsang'-ĕ.

Rope.
das Seil.
zil.

Screwdriver.
der Schraubenzieher.
shrou'-bĕn-tsee-hĕr.

Spark plugs.
die Zündkerzen.
tsünd'-ker-tsĕn.

Spring.
die Feder.
feh'-dĕr.

Starter.
der Anlasser.
an'-las-sĕr.

Steering wheel.
das Steuerrad.
stoi'-ĕr-raht.

Tail light.
das Schlusslicht.
shlus'-licHt.

Tire.
der Reifen.
ri'-fĕn.

Tube.
der Schlauch.
shloukh.

Wheel.
das Rad.
raht.

Windshield wiper.
der Scheibenwischer.
shi'-bĕn-vi-shĕr.

Wrench.
der Schraubenschlüssel.
shrou'-bĕn-shlü-sĕl.

AT THE HOTEL

I made a reservation by letter (by phone).
Ich habe brieflich (telephonisch) ein Zimmer reserviert.
iCH hah'-bĕ breef'-liCH (teh'-lĕ-foh-nish) īn tsi'-mĕr rĕ-zer'-veert.

Have you reserved a room for me?
Haben Sie für mich ein Zimmer reserviert?
hah'-bĕn zee führ miCH īn tsi'-mĕr rĕ-zer'-veert?

I reserved a single (double) room.
Ich reservierte ein Einzelzimmer (ein Doppelzimmer).
iCH rĕ-zer'-veer-tĕ īn īn'-tsĕl-tsi'-mĕr (īn do'-pĕl-tsi'-mĕr).

Do you have a room with a double bed (twin beds)?
Haben Sie ein Zimmer mit einem Doppelbett (mit zwei Betten)?
hah'-bĕn zee īn tsi'-mĕr mit i'-nem do'-pĕl-bet (mit tsvī be'-tĕn)?

Does the room have a bath?   What is the price of this room?
Ist das ein Zimmer mit Bad? Was (or: Wieviel) kostet dieses Zimmer?
ist das īn tsi'-mĕr mit baht? vas (or: vee-feel') ko'-stĕt dee'-zĕs tsi'-mĕr?

I am planning to stay ten days.
Ich beabsichtige, zehn Tage hier zu bleiben.
iCH bĕ-ap'-ziCH-ti-gĕ, tsehn tah'-gĕ heer tsoo blī'-bĕn.

The price for a single day is 25 marks.
Der Tagespreis ist fünfundzwanzig Mark.
dehr tah'-gĕs-prīs ist fünf-unt-tsvan'-tsiCH mark.

For a week we have a special rate of 150 marks.
**Für eine Woche haben wir ermässigte Preise von hundert
          fünfzig Mark.**
*führ i'-nĕ vo'-khĕ hah'-bĕn veer er-meh'-siCH-tĕ prī'-zĕ fon hun'-dĕrt-
          fünf'-tsiCH mark.*

Does that include service and tax?
Schliesst das Bedienung und Steuer ein?
shleest das bĕ-dee'-nung unt shtoi'-ĕr īn?

Do you have something less expensive?
Haben Sie ein etwas weniger teu(e)res Zimmer?
hah'-bĕn zee īn et-vas veh'-ni-gĕr toi'-(ĕ)-rĕs tsi'-mĕr?

I want a smaller (larger) room.
Ich wünsche ein kleineres (grösseres) Zimmer.
iCH vün'-shĕ īn klī'-nĕ-rĕs (gröh'-sĕ-rĕs) tsi'-mĕr.

Yes, this room will do.
Ja, dieses Zimmer ist mir recht.
yah, dee'-zĕs tsi'-mĕr ist meer reCHt.

Is breakfast included in the price?
Ist das Frühstück in dem Preis eingeschlossen?
ist das früh'-sthük in dehm prīs īn'-gĕ-shlo-sĕn?

Please have my bags carried up.
Bitte, lassen Sie mein Gepäck heraufbringen.
bi'-tĕ la'-sĕn zee mīn gĕ-pek' hĕ-rouf'-bring-ĕn.

Will you register, please?
Wollen Sie sich bitte einschreiben?
vo'-lĕn zee siCH bi'-tĕ īn'-shrī-bĕn?

Please let me have the key to my room.
Bitte, geben Sie mir meinen Zimmerschlüssel.
bi'-tĕ, geh'-bĕn zee meer mī'-nĕn tsi'-mĕr-shlü-sĕl.

Is there a washroom on the floor?
Ist eine Toilette auf dieser Etage?
ist ī'-nĕ toa-le'-tĕ ouf dee'-zĕr eh-tah'-zhĕ?

Where is the bathroom?
Wo ist das Badezimmer?
voh ist das bah'-dĕ-tsi-mĕr?

I wish to take a bath.
Ich möchte ein Bad nehmen.
iCH möCH'-tĕ īn bat neh'-mĕn.

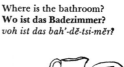

Let me know when it is ready.
Sagen Sie es mir, sobald es bereit (or: fertig) ist.
za'-gĕn zee es meer, zoh-balt' es bĕ-rīt' (or: fer'-tiCH) ist.

Bring me some more coat-hangers.
Bringen Sie mir noch einige Kleiderbügel!
bring'-ĕn zee meer nokh ī'-ni-gĕ klī'-dĕr-büh-gĕl!

Would you press a dress for me?
Wollen Sie mir ein Kleid aufbügeln?
vo'-lĕn zee meer īn klīt ouf'-büh-gĕln?

I will need it back at 7 o'clock.
Ich brauche es wieder um sieben Uhr.
iCH brou'-khĕ es vee'-dĕr um zee'-bĕn oor.

I wish to be called at 6:30 o'clock.
Ich wünsche um sechs Uhr dreissig geweckt zu werden.
iCH vün'-shĕ um zeks oor drī'-siCH gĕ-vekt tsoo vehr'-dĕn.

Have breakfast sent up at 8.
Bitte, senden Sie das Frühstück um acht Uhr herauf.
bi'-tĕ zen'-dĕn zee das früh'-shtük um akht oor hĕ-rouf'.

Where is the dining room?
Wo ist der Speisesaal (or: Wo ist das Speisezimmer)?
voh ist dehr shpī'-zĕ-zahl (or: voh ist das shpī'-sĕ-tsi-mĕr)?

I wish to have coffee and rolls.
Ich wünsche Kaffee und Brötchen.
iCH vün'-shĕ ka'-feh unt bröt'-chĕn.

I am expecting a visitor.
Ich erwarte Besuch.
iCH ĕr-var'-tĕ bĕ-zookh!

Will you please tell him to wait for me in the lobby?
Bitte, sagen Sie ihm, er möchte in der Empfangshalle auf mich warten.
bi'-tĕ, zah'-gĕn zee eem, ehr möCH'-tĕ in dehr em-pfangs'-ha-lĕ-ouf miCH var'-tĕn.

I am planning to leave tomorrow.
Ich beabsichtige, morgen abzufahren.
iCH bĕ-ap'-ziCH-ti-gĕ, mor'-gĕn ap'-tsoo-fah-rĕn.

I am going on a trip to Austria.
Ich mache eine Reise nach Österreich.
iCH ma-khĕ ī'-nĕ rī-zĕ nàhkh ö'-stĕr-rīch.

May I leave some of my baggage here?
Kann ich einiges Gepäck hier lassen?
kan iCH ī-ni-gĕs gĕ-pek' heer la'-sĕn?

I will be back on Tuesday.
Ich werde am Dienstag zurück kommen (or: zurück sein).
iCH vehr'-dĕ am deens'-tak tsoo-rük ko'-mĕn (or: ...tsoo-rük' zīn).

Please have my bill ready.
Bitte, machen Sie meine Rechnung fertig!
bi'-tĕ, ma'-khĕn zee mī'-nĕ reCH'-nung fer'-tiCH!

Would you have a taxi ready for me?
Halten Sie ein Taxi für mich bereit!
hal'-tĕn zee īn tak'-si führ mich bĕ-rīt'!

Kindly call a taxi.
Bitte, bestellen Sie ein Taxi.
bi'-tĕ, bĕ-shte'-lĕn zee īn tak'-si.

We enjoyed our stay here very much.
Unser Aufenthalt hier war sehr angenehm.
un'-zĕr ouf'-ĕnt-halt heer vahr zehr an'-gĕ-nehm.

RENTING A ROOM

Do you want a furnished or unfurnished room?
Wünschen Sie ein möbliertes oder unmöbliertes Zimmer?
wün'-shĕn zee in möh-bleer'-tĕs oh'-dĕr un'-möh-bleer-tĕs tsi'-mĕr?

I want a furnished room with (without) bath (and breakfast).
Ich möchte ein möbliertes Zimmer mit (ohne) Bad (und Frühstück).
icH möcH'-tĕ in möh-bleer'-tĕs tsi'-mĕr mit (oh'-nĕ) baht (früh-shtük).

I will eat my noon meal elsewhere.
Ich esse auswärts (or: ausserhalb) zu Mittag.
icH e'-sĕ ous'-vehrts (or: ou'-sĕr-halp) tsoo mi'-tahk.

Would you prefer a room which looks out on the street or on the sea?
**Wollen Sie ein Zimmer mit Aussicht auf die Strasse oder auf
    das Meer (or: die See)?**
*vo'-lĕn zee in tsi'-mĕr mit ou'-sicHt ouf dee shtrah'-sĕ oh'-dĕr
    ouf das mehr (or: dee zeh)?*

I shall take the one with the view of the lake.
Ich nehme das mit Aussicht auf den See.
icH neh'-mĕ das mit ou'-sicHt ouf dehn zeh.

I will be living here for some time.
Ich werde längere Zeit hier bleiben.
icH vehr'-dĕ leng'-ĕ-rĕ tsit heer bli'-bĕn.

Take all messages.
Notieren Sie alle Anrufe und Bestellungen.
noh-tee'-rĕn zee a'-lĕ an'-roo-fĕ unt bĕ-shte'-lung-ĕn.

And look after my mail.
Und sehen Sie nach meiner Post!
unt zeh'-ĕn zee nahkh mi'-nĕr post.

If friends call, (do not) show them to my room.
**Wenn Freunde kommen, bringen Sie sie (nicht) auf (or: in) mein
    Zimmer.**
ven froin'-dĕ ko'-mĕn, bri'-ngĕn zee zee (nicHt) ouf (or: in) min tsi'-mĕr.

I would like another blanket (pillow).
Ich möchte noch eine Decke (noch ein Kissen).
icH möcH'-tĕ nokh i'-nĕ de'-kĕ (ki'-sĕn).

THE SIDEWALK CAFÉ

Waiter!   A beer, please.   A Scotch whisky.
Herr Ober!   **Ein Glas Bier, bitte.**   **Einen Scotch Whisky.**
her oh'-bĕr!   *in glahs beer, bi'-tĕ.*   *i'-nĕn Skotch whisky.*

What fruit juices do you have?
Was für Obstsaft (or: Fruchtsaft) haben Sie?
vas führ ohpst'-zaft (or: frukht'-zaft) hah'-bĕn zee?

We have orange, tomato and grapefruit.
Wir haben Orangensaft, Tomatensaft und Pampelmusensaft.
*veer hah'-bĕn oh-ran'-zhĕn-zaft, toh-mah'-tĕn-zaft unt
        pam'-pĕl-moo-zĕn-zaft.*

A glass of sherry.   What kind of liqueurs do you have?
Ein Glas Sherry.   **Was für Liköre haben Sie?**
in glahs sherry.   *vas führ li-köh-rĕ hah'-bĕn zee?*

A glass of red (white) wine.   The check, please.
Ein Glas Rotwein (Weisswein).   **Die Rechnung, bitte!**
in glahs roht'-vīn (vīs'-vīn).   *dee rech'-nung, bi'-tĕ!*

DINING OUT

Can you recommend a good restaurant?
Können Sie mir ein gutes Restaurant empfehlen?
kö'-nen zee meer in goo'-tĕs re-stoh-rang' em-pfeh'-lĕn?

I would like to reserve a table for 7 o'clock.
Ich möchte einen Tisch für sieben Uhr reservieren.
ich möch'-tĕ i'-nen tish führ zee'-bĕn oor rĕ-zer-vee'-rĕn.

A table for two, please.
Einen Tisch für zwei-Personen, bitte!
i'-nĕn tish führ tsvī per-zoh'-nĕn, bi'-tĕ!

May I have a menu, please?
Darf ich um Ihre Speisekarte bitten?
darf ich um ee'-rĕ shpī'-zĕ-kar-tĕ bi'-tĕn?

What does this dish consist of?
Woraus besteht dieses Gericht (or: diese Speise)?
voh-rous' bĕ-shteht dee'-zĕs gĕ-richt (or: dee'-zĕ shpī'-zĕ)?

What is the specialty of the house?
Was ist Ihre Spezialität?
vas ist ee'-rĕ shpeh-tsi-a-li-tet'?

What do you recommend?
Was empfehlen Sie?
vas em-pfeh'-lĕn zee?

I suggest that you eat Sauerbraten.
Ich schlage vor (or: Ich empfehle), Sie essen Sauerbraten.
iCH shlah'-gĕ fohr (or: iCH em-pfeh'-lĕ), zee e'-sĕn zou'-ĕr-brah-tĕn.

Bring me a pitcher of ice water.
Bringen Sie mir einen Krug Eiswasser!
bring'-ĕn zee meer i'-nĕn krook is'-va-sĕr!

A glass of water, please.
Ein Glas Wasser, bitte!
in glahs va'-sĕr, bi'-tĕ!

My wife will have tomato juice.
Meine Frau bekommt Tomatensaft.
mi'-nĕ frou bĕ-komt' toh-ma'-tĕn-zaft.

I will start with a Ramekin (pie).
Ich beginne mit Pastete.
iCH bĕ-gi'-nĕ mit pa-steh'-tĕ.

We will take pea soup.
Wir nehmen Erbsensuppe.
veer neh'-mĕn er'-psĕn-zu-pĕ.

For the main course I would like Wiener Schnitzel.
Als Hauptgang hätte ich gern Wiener Schnitzel.
als houpt'-gang he'-tĕ iCH gern vee'-nĕr shni'-tsĕl.

Please serve us quickly. We are in a hurry.
Bitte, bedienen Sie uns schnell! Wir sind in Eile.
bi'-te, bĕ-dee'-nĕn zee uns shnel! veer zint in i'-lĕ.

Would you like something to drink, sir?
Wünschen Sie etwas zu trinken, mein Herr?
vün'-shĕn zee et'-vas tsoo tring'-kĕn, min her?

May I see the wine list.
Darf ich die Weinkarte (or: Weinliste) sehen?
darf iCH dee vin'-kar-tĕ (or: vin'-li-stĕ) zeh'-ĕn?

Which wine goes with this dish?
Welcher Wein passt zu dieser Speise?
vel'-cHĕr vin past tsoo dee'-zĕr shpi'-zĕ?

Half a bottle (or: liter) of red wine.
Eine halbe Flasche (or: Einen halben Liter) Rotwein.
i'-nĕ hal'-bĕ fla'-shĕ (or: i'-nĕn hal-bĕn lee'-tĕr) roht'-vin.

Bring me a glass of native wine.
Bringen Sie mir ein Glas Landwein!
bring'-ĕn zee meer in glahs lant'-vin!

The wine seems to be a bit sour.
Der Wein scheint ein bisschen sauer.
dehr vīn shīnt in bis'-снĕn sou'-ĕr.

Waiter, you didn't give me a napkin.
Herr Ober, Sie haben mir keine Serviette gegeben.
her oh'-bĕr, zee hah'-bĕn meer kī'-nĕ zer-vye'-tĕ ge-geh'-bĕn.

Some bread, please.
Etwas Brot, bitte.
et'-vas broht, bi'-tĕ.

Do you have any rolls?
Haben Sie Brötchen?
hah'-bĕn zee bröht-снĕn?

More butter, please.
Noch etwas Butter, bitte!
nokh et'-vas bu'-tĕr, bi'-tĕ!

Let me have ice cream for dessert.
Bringen Sie gefrorenes als Nachtisch!
bring'-ĕn zee gĕ-froh'-rĕ-nĕs als nahkh-tish!

Waiter, the check please.
Kellner (or: Ober), die Rechnung, bitte!
kel'-nĕr (or: oh'-bĕr), dee reснг'-nung, bi'-tĕ!

I think you've added this up incorrectly.
Ich glaube, Sie haben sich verrechnet.
iсн glou'-bĕ, zee hah'-bĕn ziсн vĕr-reсн'-nĕt.

I'll check it again, sir.
Ich will noch einmal nachrechnen.
iсн vil nokh'-īn'-mahl nahkh-reсн'-nĕn.

You are right. I've made a mistake.
Sie haben recht. Ich habe einen Fehler gemacht.
zee hah'-bĕn reснt. iсн hah'-bĕ ī'-nĕn feh'-lĕr gĕ-makht'.

Please pay the cashier.
Bezahlen Sie bitte an der Kasse.
bĕ-tsah'-lĕn zee bi'-tĕ an dehr ka'-sĕ.

We enjoyed the meal very much.
Das Essen hat uns sehr geschmeckt.
das e'-sĕn hat uns zehr gĕ-shmekt'.

The service was excellent.
Die Bedienung war ausgezeichnet.
dee bĕ-dee'-nung vahr ous'-gĕtsīсн-nĕt.

EAT NATIVE DISHES

This list of native dishes has been alphabetized according to their German names in order to make it easy for the tourist to read German menus.

Brook trout.
Bachforelle.
bakh'-fo-re-lĕ.

Roast chicken.
Brathuhn.
braht'-huhn.

Fried potatoes.
Bratkartoffeln.
braht-kar-to'-fĕln.

Brunswick sausage.
Braunschweiger Wurst.
broun-shvī'-gĕr vurst.

Egg pancake.
Eierpfannkuchen.
ī-ĕr-pfan-ku'-khĕn.

Roast goose.
Gänsebraten.
gen'-zĕ-brah-tĕn.

Fried meat balls.
Gebratene Frikandellen.
gĕ-brah'-te-nĕ fri'-kan-de-lĕn.

Chopped meat (Hamburger).
Gehacktes (Fleisch).
gĕ-hak'-tĕs (flīsh).

Smoked ham.
Geräucherter Schinken.
gĕ-roi'-cнĕr-tĕr shin'-kĕn.

Leg of lamb with potatoes.
Hammelkeule mit Kartoffeln.
ha'-mĕl-koi-lĕ mit kar-to'-fĕln.

Lamp chops.
Hammelkotelett.
ha'-mĕl-ko-tĕ-lĕt.

Veal cutlet a la Holstein.
Holsteiner Schnitzel.
hol-stī'-nĕr shni'-tsĕl.

Veal cutlet.
Kalbskotelett.
kalps'-ko-tĕ-lĕt.

Cold cuts.
Kalter Aufschnitt.
kal'-tĕr ouf'-shnit.

Sweet-and-sour meat balls.
Königsberger Klops.
kö'-niks-bĕr-gĕr klops.

Liver sausage.
Leberwurst.
leh'-bĕr-vurst.

Ragout, stew.
Ragout.
rah-goo'.

Sweet and sour pot roast.
Sauerbraten.
zou'-ĕr-brah-tĕn.

Ham and Eggs.
Schinken mit Eiern.
shin'-kĕn mit ī'-ĕrn.

Roast pork with red cabbage and potato dumplings.
Schweinebraten mit Rotkohl und Kartoffelklössen.
shvī'-nĕ-brah-tĕn mit rot'-kohl unt kar-to'-fĕl-klö'-sen.

Pork chops.
Schweinekotelett.
shvī'-nĕ-ko-tĕ-lĕt.

Suckling pig.
Spanferkel.
shpahn'-fer-kĕl.

Pot roast.
Schmorbraten.
shmohr'-brah-tĕn.

Veal cutlet (Viennese style).
Wiener Schnitzel.
vee'-nĕr shni'-tsĕl.

Pea soup.	Consomme.	Vegetable soup.
Erbsensuppe.	**Fleischbrühe.**	**Gemüsesuppe.**
er'-psĕn-zu-pĕ.	*flīsh'-brüh-ĕ.*	*gĕ-mü'-zĕ-zu-pĕ.*

Barley soup.	Chicken soup.	Tomato soup.
Graupensuppe.	**Hühnersuppe.**	**Tomatensuppe.**
grou'-pĕn-zu-pĕ.	*hüh'-nĕr-zu-pĕ.*	*to-mah'-tĕn-zu-pĕ.*

Apple cake.	Ice cream.	Raspberry ice.
Apfelkuchen.	**Gefrorenes.**	**Himbeereis.**
a'-pfĕl-ku-khĕn.	*gĕ-froh'-r(ĕ)-nĕs.*	*him'-behr-īs.*

Almond cake.	**Cream puffs.**	Crumb cake.
Mandeltorte.	**Mohrenköpfchen.**	**Streuselkuchen.**
man'-dĕl-tor-tĕ.	*moh'-rĕn-köpf-CHĕn.*	*shtroi'-zĕl-kuh-khĕn.*

SIGHTSEEING

I have three days to spend here.
Ich kann drei Tage hier bleiben.
iCH kan drī tah'-gĕ heer blī'-bĕn.

I would like to see the cathedral.
Ich möchte gerne die Kathedrale (or: den Dom) sehen.
iCH möCH'-tĕ gĕr'-nĕ dee ka-teh-drah'-lĕ (or: dehn dohm) zeh'-ĕn.

I also want to see some historical sites.
Ich möchte auch einige historische Plätze sehen.
iCH möCH'-tĕ oukh ī'-ni-gĕ hi-stoh'-ri-shĕ ple'-tsĕ zeh'-ĕn.

And the market places.
Und die Marktplätze.
unt dee markt'-ple-tsĕ.

Tomorrow, I want to see the night life.
Morgen beabsichtige ich, das Nachtleben kennen zu lernen.
mor'-gĕn bĕ-ap'-ziCH-ti-gĕ iCH, das nakht-leh'-bĕn ke'-nĕn tsoo ler'-nĕn.

Don't send me to any expensive places.
Empfehlen Sie mir keine zu teuren Plätze.
ĕm-pfeh'-lĕn zee meer kī'-nĕ tsoo toi'-rĕn ple'-tsĕ.

Here are a few I want to see.
Hier sind einige, die ich besuchen will.
heer zint ī'-ni-gĕ, dee iCH bĕ-zookh'-ĕn vil.

Can we make a tour of these places?
Können wir eine Tour dieser Plätze machen?
kö'-nĕn veer ī'-nĕ toor dee'-zĕr ple'-tsĕ makh'-ĕn?

Let me know when we get to each.
Sagen Sie mir, wenn wir zu jedem kommen.
zah'-gĕn zee meer, ven veer tsoo yeh'-dĕm ko'-mĕn.

Let me know what they are.
Sagen Sie mir, was für Plätze es sind.
zah'-gĕn zee meer, vas führ ple'-tsĕ es zint.

I want to see the most important things.
Ich möchte die wichtigsten Dinge sehen.
iсн möсн'-tĕ dee viсн'-tik-stĕn ding'-ĕ zeh'-ĕn.

I want to spend more time here.
Ich möchte länger hier bleiben.
iсн möсн'-tĕ leng'-ĕr heer blī'-bĕn.

I think I've seen enough. I am tired.
Ich denke, ich habe genug gesehen. Ich bin müde.
iсн dĕng'-kĕ, iсн hah'-bĕ gĕ-nook' gĕ-zeh'-ĕn. iсн bin mü'-dĕ.

I would like to return to my hotel.
Ich möchte gern ins Hotel zurückkehren.
iсн möснtĕ gern ins hoh-tel' tsoo-rük'-keh-rĕn.

SNAPSHOTS FOR REMEMBRANCE

Would you mind letting me take your picture?
Würden Sie mir erlauben, eine Aufnahme von Ihnen zu machen?
vür'-dĕn zee meer ĕr-lou'-bĕn, ī'-nĕ ouf'-nah-mĕ fon ee'-nĕn tsoo ma'-khĕn?

Just continue your work.
Fahren Sie nur mit Ihrer Arbeit fort!
fah'-rĕn zee noor mit ee'-rĕr ar'-bīt fort!

Don't look into the camera.
Blicken Sie nicht in den Apparat!
bli'-kĕn zee niснt in dehn a-pa-raht!

Turn this way, please.
Wenden Sie sich bitte nach dieser Seite!
ven'-dĕn zee ziсн bi'-tĕ nakh dee'-zĕr zī-tĕ!

Thank you very much for your trouble.
Ich danke Ihnen vielmals für Ihre Mühe.
ich dang'-kĕ ee'-nĕn feel'-mahls führ ee'-rĕ müh'-ĕ.

I'd like you to have this for your trouble.
Ich möchte Ihnen das für Ihre Mühe geben.
iCH möCH'-te ee'-nĕn das führ ee'-rĕ müh'-ĕ geh'-bĕn.

I would like a roll of film, number 620.
Ich möchte einen Rollfilm, Nummer sechshundertzwanzig.
iCH möCH'-tĕ ĭ'-nĕn rol'-film nu'-mĕr zeks'-hun'-dĕrt-tsvan'-tsiCH.

Do you have color film?
Haben Sie Farbfilm?
hah'-bĕn zee farp'-film?

Will you load the camera for me, please?
Würden Sie mir bitte den Film einspannen?
wür'-dĕn zee meer bi'-tĕ dehn film in'-shpa-nĕn?

The shutter is stuck. Will you please look at it?
Der Verschluss klemmt. Wollen Sie bitte nachsehen?
dehr fĕr-shlus' klemt. vo'-lĕn zee bi'-tĕ nahkh'-zeh-ĕn?

Why does my film get scratched?
Wie kommt es, dass mein Film zerkratzt wurde?
vee komt es, das mīn film tsĕr-kratst vur'-dĕ?

Do you think I should use a filter?
Meinen Sie, dass ich einen Filter benutzen soll?
mĭ'-nĕn zee, das iCH ĭ'-nen fil'-tĕr bĕ-nu'-tsĕn zol?

Please develop this roll.
Bitte, entwickeln Sie diese Rolle (or: **diesen Film**).
bi'-tĕ, ĕnt-vi'-kĕln zee dee'-zĕ ro'-lĕ (or: *dee'-zĕn film*).

Please make one print of each negative.
Bitte, machen Sie eine Kopie für jedes Negativ!
bi'-tĕ, ma'-khĕn zee ĭ'-nĕ ko-pee' führ yeh'-dĕs neh'-ga-teef!

When will it be ready?
Wann ist es fertig?
van ist es fer'-tiCH?

Do you sell flashbulbs?
Verkaufen Sie Blitzlichtbirnen?
fĕr-kou'-fĕn zee blits-liCHt-bir-nĕn?

SHOPPING WITH ASSURANCE

Where are the main department stores?
Wo sind die bedeutendsten Kaufhäuser (or: Waren . . .)?
voh zint dee bĕ-doi'-tĕnt-stĕn kouf'-hoi-zĕr (or: vahr'-rĕn . . .)?

Is it too far to walk?
Ist es zu weit, dorthin zu Fuss zu gehen?
ist es tsoo vit, dort'-hin tsoo foos tsoo geh'-ĕn?

What number bus (trolley) will take me there?
Welcher Autobus (Welche Strassenbahn) wird mich hinbringen?
*vel'-cHĕr ou'-toh-bus (vel'-chĕ shtrah'-sĕn-bahn) virt micH
    hin'-bring-ĕn?*

Good morning. May I look at your merchandise?
Guten Morgen! Darf ich mir Ihre Ware ansehen?
goo'-tĕn mor'-gĕn! darf icH meer ee'-rĕ vah'-rĕ an'-zeh-ĕn?

Would you show me one of these?
Wollen Sie mir einen (or: eine, eins) davon zeigen?
vo'-len zee meer ī'-nen (or: ī'-nĕ, īns) da-fon tsī'-gĕn?

Where was it made?
Wo wurde er (or: sie, es) gemacht?
voh vur'-dĕ ehr (or: zee, es) gĕ-makht?

Let me see that.
Zeigen Sie mir das!
tsī'-gĕn zee meer das?

I would like to see a dress (suit, skirt, blouse, slip, nightgown,
    gloves, hat).
**Ich möchte ein Kleid (ein Kostüm, einen Rock, eine Bluse,
    ein Unterkleid, ein Nachthemd, ein Paar Handschuhe,
    einen Hut) sehen.**
*icH möcH'-tĕ īn klīt (ko-stüm', rok, bloo'-zĕ, un'-tĕr-klīt, nakht'-hemt,
    pahr hant'-shoo-ĕ, hoot) zeh'-ĕn.*

I need a suit (trousers, jacket, overcoat, shirt, necktie, socks, shoes).
**Ich brauche einen Anzug (eine Hose, eine Jacke, einen Mantel, ein
    Hemd, eine Krawatte, Socken, Schuhe).**
*icH brou'-khĕ ī'-nĕn an'-tsook (hoh'-zĕ, ja'-kĕ, man'-tĕl, hemt,
    krah-va'-tĕ, zo'-kĕn, shoo'-ĕ).*

This is too small (large).
Das ist zu klein (gross).
das ist tsoo klīn (grohs).

That is too tight (loose).
Das ist zu eng (lose).
das ist tsoo eng (loh'-zĕ).

Do you have this in a lighter (darker) color?
Haben Sie das in einer helleren (dunkleren) Farbe?
hah'-běn zee das in ĭ'-něr he'-lě-rěn (dun'-klě-rěn) far'-be?

Have you something better?
Haben Sie etwas besseres?
hah'-běn zee et'-vas be'sě-rěs?

What material is it made of?
Aus was für einem Material besteht es?
ous vas führ ĭ'-něm ma-teh-ri-ahl' bě-shteht' es?

How much is it?
Wieviel kostet es?
vee-feel' ko'-stět es?

That is fine. Please wrap it up.
Das ist schön. Bitte, packen Sie es ein.
das ist shöhn. bi'-tě, pa'-kěn žee es ĭn.

Please send it to my hotel.
Bitte, senden Sie es zu meinem Hotel.
bi'-tě zen'-děn zee es tsoo mĭ'-nem hoh-těl'.

I will take it with me.
Ich nehme es mit.
ĭCH neh'-měs es mit.

Please let me have a sales slip.
Bitte, geben Sie mir eine Quittung.
bi'-tě, geh'-běn zee meer ĭ'-ne kvi'-tung.

I would like to have this shipped to my home.
Ich möchte das an meine Heimatadresse versandt haben.
ĭCH möCH'-tě das an mĭ'-ne hĭ'-maht-a-dre'-sě fěr-zant' hah'-běn.

How much is this a yard (a meter)?
Wieviel kostet das per Elle (per Meter)?
vee-feel' ko'-stět das pěr e'-lě (per meh'-těr)?

What do you have for a five-year-old?
Was haben Sie für eine(n) Fünfjährige(n)?
vas hah'-běn zee führ ĭ'-ně(n) fünf'-yeh-ri-gě(n)?

Do you have embroidered dresses?
Haben Sie Kleider mit Stickerei?
hah'-běn zee klĭ'-der mit shti'-kě-rī?

What is the price of that suede jacket?
Was kostet diese Wildlederjacke?
vas ko'-stět dee'-ze vilt'-leh-děr-ya-kě?

In what country was it made?
In welchem Land wurde sie gemacht?
in vel'-CHěm lant vur'-dě zee gě-makht'?

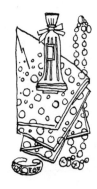

Let me see a silk dress.   Do you have my size in green?
Zeigen Sie mir ein Seidenkleid! Haben Sie meine Grösse in grün?
tsī'-gĕn zee meer in zī'-dĕn-klīt! hah'-bĕn zee mī'-ne gröh'-sĕ in grühn?

I like the black rayon one.
Mir gefällt das aus schwarzer Kunstseide.
meer gĕ-felt' das ous shvar'-tsĕr koonst'-zī-dĕ.

How long is the bright red one?   Do you have this shirt in blue?
Wie lang ist das hellrote?   **Haben Sie dieses Hemd in blau?**
vee lang ist das hel roh'-tĕ?   *hah'-bĕn zee dee'-zĕs hemt in blou?*

Where is the leather goods counter?
Wo ist die Lederwarenabteilung?
voh ist dee leh'-dĕr-vah-rĕn-ap-tī-lung?

On the second floor.[1]
Im zweiten Stock (or: In der zweiten Etage).
im tsvī'-tĕn shtok (or: in dehr tsvī'-tĕn eh-tah'-zhĕ).

What is the price of that alligator handbag?
Was kostet diese Alligatorhandtasche?
vas ko'-stĕt dee'-ze a-li-gah'-tohr-hant-ta-shĕ?

I will take this belt.   I want to buy a pair of shoes.
Ich nehme diesen Gürtel.   **Ich will ein Paar Schuhe kaufen.**
ıcн neh'-mĕ dee'-zĕn gür'-tĕl.   *ıcн vil in pahr shoo'-ĕ kou'-fĕn.*

Which color do you like: black, brown, or white?
Welche Farbe wünschen Sie? Schwarz, braun oder weiss?
vel'-cнĕ far'-bĕ vün'-shĕn zee? shvarts, broun oh'-dĕr vīs?

I would like to see a pair of brown shoes.
Ich möchte ein Paar braune Schuhe sehen.
ıcн möcн'-tĕ in pahr brou'-nĕ shoo'-hĕ zeh'-ĕn.

I am afraid these would not fit you, sir. They are too narrow and
     also too short.
Ich glaube, diese werden Ihnen nicht passen, mein Herr.
     Sie sind zu eng und auch zu kurz.
ıcн glau'-bĕ, dee'-zĕ vehr'-dĕn ee'-nĕn nıcнt pa'-sĕn, mīn her.
     zee zint tsoo eng unt aukh tsoo kurts.

---

[1] Europeans do not count the ground floor. The second floor would,
therefore, be called the first floor and the third would be the second.

You are right. I need a larger size.
Sie haben recht. Ich brauche eine grössere Nummer.
zee hah'-bĕn rᴇcнт. ιcн brou'-khĕ ĭ'-nĕ gröh'-sĕ-rĕ nu'-mĕr.

What is the price of this perfume?
Was kostet dieses Parfum?
vas ko'-stĕt dee'-zĕs par-fühng'?

Do you have a smaller (larger) bottle?
Haben Sie eine kleinere (grössere) Flasche?
hah'-bĕn zee ĭ'-nĕ klī'-nĕ-rĕ (gröh'-sĕ-rĕ) fla'-shĕ?

What is the price of these earrings?
Was kosten diese Ohrringe?
vas ko'-stĕn dee'-zĕ ohr'-ring-ĕ?

Let me see that bracelet, please.
Zeigen Sie mir bitte dieses Armband.
tsī'-gĕn zee meer bi'-tĕ dee'-zĕs arm'-bant.

Show me a silver tray.
Zeigen Sie mir ein silbernes Tablett!
tsī'-gĕn zee meer ĭn zil'-bĕr-nĕs ta-blet'!

You make silver articles to order, don't you?
**Stimmt es, dass Sie Silbersachen nach Angaben oder
        Vorlagen anfertigen?**
*shtimt es, das zee zil'-bĕr-zakh-ĕn nahkh an'-gah-bĕn oh'-dĕr
        fohr'-lah-gĕn an'-fer-ti-gĕn?*

LAUNDRY AND CLEANING

Please have this dry cleaned.
Bitte, lassen Sie das chemisch reinigen.
bi'-tĕ, la'-sĕn zee das cнeh'-mish rī'-ni-gĕn.

How long will it take?
Wie lange dauert es?
vee lang'-ĕ dou'-ĕrt es?

I would like this suit pressed.
Ich möchte gern diesen Anzug aufgebügelt haben.
ιcн möcн'-tĕ gern dee'-zen an'-tsook ouf'-gĕ-büh-gĕlt hah'-bĕn.

Can I get it back this afternoon?
Kann ich ihn heute Nachmittag wieder zurück haben?
kan icH een hoi'-tě nahkh'-mi-tahk vee'-děr tsoo-rük' hah'-běn?

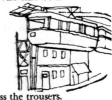

These shirts need laundering.
Diese Hemden müssen gewaschen werden.
dee'-zě hem'-děn mü'-sěn gě-va'-shěn vehr'-děn.

Please do not starch them.
Keine Stärke, bitte.
ki'-ně shter'-kě, bi'-tě.

Please wash this dress.
Bitte, waschen Sie dieses Kleid.
bi'-tě, va'-shěn zee dee'-zěs klit.

Please press the trousers.
Bitte, bügeln Sie die Hosen.
bi'-tě, büh'-gěln zee dee hoh'-zěn.

When can you have it ready?
Wann werden sie fertig sein?
van vehr'děn zee fer'-ticH zin?

I must have it tomorrow.
Ich muss sie (or: es) morgen haben.
icH mus zee (or: es) mor'-gěn hah'-běn.

Can you sew a button on my shirt?
Können Sie an meinem Oberhemd einen Knopf annähen?
kö'-něn zee an mi'-něm oh'-běr-hemt i'-něn knopf an'-neh-ěn?

This is torn. Can you mend it?
Das ist zerrissen. Können Sie es flicken?
das ist tse-ri'-sěn. kö'-něn zee es fli'-kěn?

HAIRDRESSERS AND BARBERS

Could you direct me to a good hairdresser?
Können Sie mir einen guten Friseur empfehlen?
kö'-něn zee meer i'-něn goo'-těn free-zöhr' ěm-pfeh'-lěn?

I would like to have my hair washed and set.
Ich möchte meine Haare gewaschen und frisiert haben.
icH möcH-tě mi'-ně hah'-rě gě-va'-shěn unt free-zeert' hah'-běn.

Would you like a permanent wave?
Wünschen Sie eine Dauerwelle?
vün'-shěn zee i'-ne dou'-ěr-ve-lě?

What is the charge?
Wieviel kostet es?
vee-feel' ko'-stět es?

I would like a haircut, please.
Haarschneiden, bitte.
hahr'-shni-děn, bi'-tě.

I want a crew cut.
Ganz kurz, bitte.
gants kurts, bi'-tě.

Not too much off the top.
Nicht zu viel von oben abschneiden.
niCHt tsoo feel fon oh'-bĕn ap'-shnī-dĕn.

Cut it shorter, please.
Kürzer, bitte.
kür'-tsĕr, bi'-tĕ.

I would like to make an appointment for a manicure.
Ich möchte mich zum Maniküren anmelden.
iCH möcH-tĕ miCH tsoom mah-ni-küh'-rĕn an'-mel-dĕn.

What time can you take me for a shampoo?
Wann können Sie mir die Haare waschen?
van kö'-nĕn zee meer dee hah'-rĕ vash'-ĕn?

I want to have a shave.
Rasieren, bitte.
rah-zee'-rĕn, bi'-tĕ.

GOING TO CHURCH

I would like to go to church.
Ich möchte zur Kirche gehen.
iCH möcH'-tĕ tsoor kir'-CHĕ geh'-ĕn.

Where is the (nearest) church?
Wo ist die (nächste) Kirche?
voh ist dee (nehkh'-stĕ) kir'-CHĕ?

Where is the cathedral?
Wo ist der Dom?
voh ist dehr dohm?

Where is the synagogue?
Wo ist die Synagoge?
voh ist dee zü-na-goh'-gĕ?

What kind of a church is this?
Was für eine Kirche ist das?
vas führ ī'-nĕ kir'-CHĕ ist das?

A Catholic church.
Eine katholische Kirche.
ī'-nĕ ka-toh'-li-shĕ kir'-CHe.

A Protestant church.
Eine protestantische Kirche.
ī'-nĕ pro-te-stan'-ti-shĕ hir'-CHĕ.

At what time does the service start?
Wann beginnt der Gottesdienst?
van bĕ-gint' dehr go'-tĕs-deenst?

What church holds service in English?
Welche Kirche hält den Gottesdienst in englisch ab?
vel'-CHĕ kir'-CHe helt dehn go'-tĕs-deenst in eng'-lish ap?

I would like to see the minister (priest, rabbi).
Ich möchte den Pastor (Priester, Rabbiner) sprechen.
iCH möcH'-tĕ dehn pa-stohr' (pree'-stĕr, ra-bee'-nĕr) shpre'-CHĕn.

THEATER GOING

I should like two tickets for Faust.
Ich möchte zwei Karten (or: Eintrittskarten) für Faust haben.
iCH *möCH'-tĕ tsvī kar'-tĕn* (or: *īn'-trits-kar-tĕn*) *führ foust hah'-bĕn.*

Have you any seats for tonight?
Haben Sie Sitzplätze für heute abend?
hah'-bĕn zee zits'-ple-tsĕ führ hoi'-tĕ ah'-bĕnt?

Where are the seats?
Wo sind die Sitze?
voh zint dee zi'-tsĕ?

Can you show me a seating plan of the theater?
Können Sie mir einen Sitzplan des Theaters zeigen?
kö'-nĕn zee meer ī'-nĕn zits'-plahn des teh-ah'-ters tsī'-gĕn?

Please let me have 2 orchestra (mezzanine, box, balcony) seats.
Bitte geben Sie mir zwei Parkettsitze (erste Balkon sitze, Logen sitze, zweite Balkon sitze).
bi'-tĕ geh'-bĕn zee meer tsvī pahr-ket'-zi-tsĕ (ehr'-stĕ bal-kong'-zi-tsĕ, loh'-zhĕn-zi-tsĕ, tsvī'-tĕ bal-kong'-zi-tsĕ).

At what time does the performance start?
Um wieviel Uhr (Wann) beginnt die Vorstellung?
um vee-feel' oor (van) bĕ-gint' dee fohr-shte-lung?

NIGHT LIFE

I want to visit several night clubs.
Ich will mehrere Nachtlokale besuchen.
iCH *vil meh'-rĕ-rĕ nakht'-loh-kah-lĕ bĕ-zookh'-ĕn.*

I am interested in seeing some good floor shows.
Ich möchte mir gerne einige gute Revuen ansehen.
iCH *möCH'-tĕ meer ger'-nĕ ī'-ni-gĕ goo'-tĕ rĕ-vüh'-ĕn an'-zeh-ĕn.*

What places do you recommend?
Welche empfehlen Sie?
vel'-CHĕ em-pfeh'-lĕn zee?

Are they very expensive?
Sind sie sehr teuer?
zint zee zehr toi'ĕr?

Is there a cover charge?
Gibt es einen Minimumpreis?
gipt es ī-nĕn mi'-ni-mum-prīs?

Are there any other charges?
Gibt es noch andere Kosten?
gipt es nokh an'-dĕ-rĕ ko'-stĕn?

What time does the floor show start?
Wann (or: Um wieviel Uhr) fängt die Vorstellung an?
van (or: um vee-feel' oor) fengt dee fohr'-shte-lung an?

There is an error in the bill.
Es ist ein Irrtum in der Rechnung.
es ist īn ir'-toom in dehr RECH*'-nung.*

Please see that my bill is corrected.
Lassen Sie bitte meine Rechnung richtigstellen.
la'-sĕn zee bi'-tĕ mī'-nĕ RECH*'-nung* RICH*'-tiCH-shte'-lĕn.*

EXCHANGING MONEY

What is today's free market rate on the dollar?
Was ist der heutige Kurs des Dollars im Freihandel?
vas ist dehr hoi'-ti-gĕ kurs des do'-lahrs im frī'-han-dĕl?

We do not pay anything but the legal rate.
Wir zahlen bloss nach dem offiziellen Kurs.
veer tsah'-lĕn blohs nahkk dehm o-fi-tsie'-lĕn kurs.

What have you got? Dollars or travelers' checks?
Was haben Sie? Dollar oder Reiseschecks?
vas hah'-bĕn zee? do'-lahr oh'-dĕr rī'-zĕ-sheks?

I would like to cash a travelers' check.
Ich möchte einen Reisescheck einwechseln (or: einlösen).
iCH möCH'-tĕ ī'-nĕn rī-zĕ-shek īn'-vek-zĕln (or: īn'-löh-zĕn).

May I have 10 marks in small notes?
Kann ich zehn Mark in niedrigen Geldscheinen haben?
kan iCH tsehn mark in nee'-drig-ĕn gelt'-shī-nĕn hah'-bĕn?

Please change this note for me.
Bitte, wechseln Sie mir diesen Geldschein.
bi'-tĕ, vek-zĕln zee meer dee'-zĕn gelt'-shīn.

Where can I buy a bank draft?
Wo kann ich einen Bankscheck kaufen?
voh kan iCH ī'-nĕn bangk'-shek kou'-fĕn?

I would like to send a draft for 250 marks.
Ich möchte einen Bankscheck für zweihundertfünfzig Mark senden.
iCH möCH'-tĕ ī'-nĕn bangh'-shek führ tsvī-hun-dĕrt-fünf'-tsiCH mark
    zen'-dĕn.

COMMUNICATIONS

Mail

Where is the (nearest) post office?
Wo ist das (nächste) Postamt?
voh ist das (nehkh'-stĕ) post'-amt?

Until what time is it open?
Wie lange ist es offen?
vee lang'-ĕ ist es o'-fĕn?

It closes at five o'clock.
Es schliesst um fünf Uhr.
es shleest um fünf oor.

Where can I buy some stamps?
Wo kann ich Briefmarken kaufen?
voh kan ich breef-mar-kĕn kou'-fĕn?

Which window do I go to for airmail?
Welcher Schalter ist für Luftpost?
vel'-chĕr shal'-tĕr ist für luft'-post?

Let me have an airmail stamp, please.
Bitte, geben Sie mir eine Luftpostmarke.
bi'-tĕ, geh'-bĕn zee meer ī'-nĕ luft'-post-mar-kĕ.

Where can I drop these letters?
Wo kann ich diese Briefe einwerfen?
voh kan ich dee'-zĕ bree'-fĕ īn'-ver-fĕn?

I want to send this special delivery.
Ich möchte das per Eilpost senden.
ich möch'-tĕ das pĕr īl'-post zen'-dĕn.

How much postage do I need for this letter?
Wieviel Porto brauche ich für diesen Brief?
vee-feel' por'-toh brou'-khĕ ich führ dee'-zĕn breef?

I would like to register this letter.
Ich möchte diesen Brief einschreiben lassen.
ich möch'-tĕ dee'-zĕn breef īn'-shrī-bĕn la'-sĕn.

I would like ten post cards.
Ich möchte zehn Postkarten haben.
ich möch'-tĕ tsehn post'-kar-tĕn hah'-bĕn.

May I insure this parcel?
Kann ich dieses Paket versichern lassen?
kan ich dee'-zĕs pa-keht fĕr-zich'-ĕrn la'-sĕn?

What does it contain?
Was enthält es?
vas ent-helt es?

Books and printed matter.
Bücher und Drucksachen.
büh'-chĕr unt drukh'-za-khĕn.

Hold my mail until I call for it.
Heben Sie meine Post auf, bis ich sie abhole!
heh'-bĕn zee mī'-nĕ post ouf, bis ich zee ap'-hoh-lĕ!

Please forward my mail to Munich.
Bitte, leiten Sie meine Post nach München weiter.
bi'-tĕ, lī'-tĕn zee mī'-ne post nahkh mün'-chĕn vī'-tĕr.

Don't bother to send magazines and newspapers.
Senden Sie keine Zeitschriften und Zeitungen!
zen'-dĕn zee kī'-nĕ tsīt-shrif-tĕn unt tsī'-tung-ĕn!

Telegrams and Cables

I would like to send a telegram to Düsseldorf.
Ich möchte ein Telegramm nach Düsseldorf aufgeben (or: senden).
ich möch'-tĕ īn teh-le-gram' nahkh Dü'-sel-dorf ouf'-geh-bĕn (or: zen'-dĕn).

How much do fifteen words cost?
Wieviel kosten fünfzehn Worte?
vee-feel' ko'-stĕn fünf-tsehn vor'-tĕ?

Send it immediately.
Senden Sie es sofort!
zen'-dĕn zee es zoh-fort'!

Are you sending it day rate or night rate?
Senden Sie es zum Tagespreis oder zum Nachtpreis?
zen'-dĕn zee es tsum tah'-gĕs-prīs oh'-dĕr tsum nakht'-prīs?

Telephoning

Where is the telephone (the telephone book)?
Wo ist das Telefon (das Telefonbuch)?
voh ist das teh-lĕ-fohn' (das teh-lĕ-fohn'-bookh)?

Operator, I have dialed the wrong number.
Fräulein, ich habe die falsche Nummer gewählt.
froi'-līn ich hah'-bĕ dee fal'-shĕ nu'-mĕr gĕ-velt'.

This is Mr. Winter calling.
Hier ist Herr Winter.
heer ist her vin'-tĕr.

May I speak to Mr. (Mrs., Miss) Brown?
Kann ich Herrn (Frau, Fräulein) Braun sprechen?
kan ich hern (frou, froi'-līn) broun shpre'-chĕn?

No, he (she) is not in.
Nein, er (sie) ist nicht zu Hause.
nīn, ehr (zee) ist nicht tsoo hou'-zĕ.

When do you expect him (her)?
Wann erwarten Sie ihn (sie)?
van ĕr-var'-tĕn zee een (zee)?

Hold the wire, please. I'll put him on.
Einen Augenblick, bitte. Ich verbinde Sie.
i'-nĕn ou'-gĕn-blik, bi'-tĕ. ich fĕr-bin'-dĕ zee.

I want to make a long distance call.
Ich will ein Ferngespräch machen.
ich vil in fern'-gĕ-shprech makh'-ĕn.

This is a station-to-station call.
Dies ist ein einfacher Anruf.
dees ist in in'-fa-khĕr an'-roof.

I would like to call Chicago at 3:00.
Ich möchte Chicago um drei Uhr anrufen.
ich möch'-tĕ Chicago um drī oor an'-roo-fĕn.

How much is a call to New York?
Wieviel kostet ein Gespräch mit New York?
vee-feel' ko'-stĕt in gĕ-shprech mit New York?

I am sorry. All the lines are busy.
Ich bedaure (or: Es tut mir leid). Alle Leitungen sind besetzt.
ich bĕ-dou'-rĕ (or: es toot meer līt). a'-lĕ lī'-tung-ĕn zint bĕ-zetst'.

Tell him (her) Mr. Lehmann is calling.
Sagen Sie ihm (ihr), dass Herr Lehmann anruft.
zah'-gĕn ze eem (eer), das her leh'-man an'-rooft.

Signal me when the three minutes are over.
Unterbrechen Sie mich, wenn drei Minuten vorbei sind!
un-tĕr-bre'-chĕn zee mich, ven drī mee-noo'-tĕn fohr-bī zint!

Please do not interrupt.
Bitte, unterbrechen Sie mich nicht.
bi'-tĕ, un-tĕr-brech'-ĕn zee mich nicht.

TOURIST INFORMATION

Where is the nearest travel agency?
Wo ist das nächste Reisebüro?
voh ist das nehkh'-stĕ rī'-zĕ-büh-roh?

When does the next bus leave for Nürnberg?
Wann fährt der nächste Bus nach Nürnberg?
van fehrt dehr nehkh'-stĕ bus nahkh nürn'-berk?

What local food do you recommend?
Welches Nationalgericht empfehlen Sie?
*vel'-*CHĕ*s na-tsio-nahl'-gĕ-richt ĕm-pfeh'-lĕn zee?*

I wish to visit a place where there are no tourists.
Ich möchte einen Ort besuchen, wo sich keine Touristen aufhalten.
     (or: wo keine Touristen sind).
ich möch'-te ĭ'-nĕn ort bĕ-zookh'-ĕn, voh zich kĭ'-nĕ too-ri'-stĕn
     ouf'-hal-tĕn (or: vo kĭ'-nĕ too-ri'-stĕn zint).

I have many choices.
Ich habe eine grosse Auswahl.
ich hah'-bĕ ĭ'-nĕ groh'-sĕ ous'-vahl.

Is this town off the beaten track (little frequented by tourists)?
Ist dies ein ruhiges Dorf (Städtchen) mit wenig Fremdenverkehr?
*ist dees in roo'-i-gĕs dorf (shtet'-*CHĕ*n) mit veh'-nich*
     frem'-dĕn-fĕr-kehr?

Yes, very much so.	Is it difficult to reach?
Ja, ganz gewiss.	**Ist es schwer zu erreichen?**
yah, gants gĕ-vis'.	*ist es shvehr tsoo e-rĭ'-*CHĕ*n?*

No, there is frequent bus service.
Nein, es gibt da einen häufigen Autobusdienst.
nĭn, es gipt dah ĭ'-nen hoi'-fi-gĕn ou'-toh-bus-deenst.

Does it have a good, inexpensive hotel?
Gibt es da ein gutes, billiges Hotel?
gipt es dah in goo'-tĕs, bi'-li-gĕs hoh-tel'?

Certainly. We recommend the Hotel Metropole.
Gewiss. Wir empfehlen das Hotel Metropole.
gĕ-vis. veer ĕm-pfeh'-lĕn das hoh-tel' meh'-tro-pol.

YOUR HEALTH ABROAD

I have an upset stomach.	I don't feel well.
Ich habe mir den Magen verdorben.	**Ich fühle mich nicht wohl.**
ɪch *hah'-bĕ meer den mah'-gĕn*	ɪch *füh'-lĕ* mɪch *nɪcht vohl.*
fĕr-dor'-bĕn.	

I need a doctor (dentist, occulist) who speaks English.
Ich brauche einen Arzt (Zahnarzt, Augenarzt), der englisch spricht.
ɪch *brou'-khĕ ĭ'-nĕn ahrtst (tsahn'-ahrtst, ou'-gĕn-ahrtst),*
     dehr eng'-lish shpricht.

I cut myself.
Ich habe mich geschnitten.
iCH hah'-bĕ miCH gĕ-shnit'-ĕn.

I have a bad cold.
Ich habe mich schwer erkältet.
iCH hah'-bĕ miCH shvehr ĕr-kel'-tĕt.

I have sprained (broken) my foot.
Ich habe mir den Fuss verstaucht (gebrochen).
iCH hah'-bĕ meer den fus fĕr-stoukht' (gĕ-bro-khĕn).

Where does it hurt?
Wo schmerzt es?
voh shmertst es?

I have a fever.
Ich habe Fieber.
iCH hah'-bĕ fee'-bĕr.

Will I have to stay in bed?
Muss ich im Bett bleiben?
mus iCH im bet blī'-bĕn?

My back (foot) hurts.
Mein Rücken (Fuss) tut weh.
mīn rü'-kĕn (fuhs) toot veh.

What is your fee, doctor?
Herr Doktor, was ist Ihr Honorar?
her dok'-tohr, vas ist eer hoh-noh-rahr'?

I have a toothache.
Ich habe Zahnschmerzen.
iCH hah'-bĕ tsahn'-shmer-tsĕn.

Must the tooth be filled?
Muss mein Zahn plombiert werden?
mus mīn tsahn plom-beert vehr'-dĕn?

Will the tooth have to be extracted?
Muss der Zahn gezogen werden?
mus dehr tsahn gĕ-tsoh'-gen vehr'-dĕn?

Where is the nearest drugstore?
Wo ist die nächste Apotheke?
voh ist dee nehCH'-stĕ a-poh-teh'-kĕ?

Can you fill this prescription?
Können Sie dieses Rezept anfertigen?
kö'-nen zee dee'-zĕs reh-tsept' an'-fĕr-ti-gĕn?

When will it be ready?
Wann wird es fertig sein?
van virt es fer'-tiCH zīn?

I will come back to pick it up.
Ich komme zurück, um es abzuholen.
iCH ko'-mĕ tsoo-rük, um es ap'-tsoo-hoh-lĕn.

I have broken my glasses.
Ich habe meine Brille zerbrochen.
iCH hah'-bĕ mī'-nĕ bri'-lĕ tser-bro'-khĕn.

Can you put in a new lens?
Können Sie ein neues Augenglas einsetzen?
kö'-nĕn zee īn noi'-ĕs ou'-gen-glahs īn'-zets-ĕn?

SPORTS

Swimming and Bathing

Can I rent a suit (trunks)?
Kann ich mir einen Badeanzug (eine Badehose) ausleihen?
kan ich meer ī'-nĕn bah'-dĕ-an-tsook (īne bah'-dĕ-hoh-zĕ) ous'-lī-ĕn?

Is the pool chlorinated?
Ist das Schwimmwasser chloriniert?
ist das shvim'-va-sĕr khloh-ree-neert?

I would like to rent a towel.
Ich möchte mir ein Handtuch ausleihen.
ich möch'-tĕ meer in han'-tukh ous'-līhĕn.

Is the towel included in the price of admission?
Ist das Handtuch im Eintrittspreis eingeschlossen?
ist das han'-tukh im in'-trits-prīs in'-gĕ-shlo-sĕn?

Do you have suntan oil?
Haben Sie Öl gegen Sonnenbrand?
hah'-bĕn zee öhl geh'-gĕn zo'-nĕn-brant?

I would like to rent a cabin.
Ich möchte eine Kabine mieten.
ich möch'-tĕ ī'-nĕ kah-bee'-nĕ mee'-tĕn.

On the Golf Course

I would like to rent a set of golf clubs, please.
Ich möchte mir einen Satz Golfschläger ausleihen.
ich möch-tĕ meer ī'-nĕn zats golf'-shleh-gĕr ous'-lī-ĕn.

Will you provide me with a good caddy?
Besorgen Sie mir einen guten Köcherträger?
bĕ-zor'-gĕn zee meer ī'-nĕn goo'-tĕn kö-chĕr-treh-gĕr?

I wish to buy some golf balls.   Where do I tee off?
Ich will einige Golfbälle kaufen.   **Wo beginne ich das Golfspiel?**
ich vil ī'-ni-gĕ golf'-be-lĕ kou'-fĕn.   *voh bĕ-gi'-nĕ ich das golf'-shpeel?*

Caddy, my driver, please.
Köcherträger, meinen ersten Golfschläger, bitte.
kö-chĕn-treh-gĕr, mī'-nĕn ehr'-stĕn golf'-shleh-gĕr, bi'-tĕ.

At the Tennis Courts

What is the charge for the use of the courts?
Was kostet die Benutzung der Tennisplätze?
vas ko'-stĕt dee bĕ-nu'-tsung dehr te'-nis-pleh'-tsĕ?

Can I have a racket?
Kann ich einen Tennisschläger haben?
kan ıсн ī'-nĕn te'-nis-shleh-gĕr hah'-bĕn?

I would like to buy a can of balls.
Ich möchte eine Büchse Bälle kaufen.
ıсн möсн-tĕ ī'-nĕ bükh'-zĕ be'-lĕ kou'-fĕn.

Where is the men's locker room?
Wo ist der Anziehraum für Männer?
voh ist dehr an'-tsee-roum führ me'-nĕr?

Fishing and Hunting

I need a rod and reel, some line, and hooks.
Ich brauche eine Angelrute mit Roller, Schnur und Angelhaken.
ıсн brou'-khĕ ī'-nĕ ang'-ĕl-roo-tĕ mit ro'-ler, shnoor unt ang'-ĕl-hah-kĕn.

Where can I rent a boat?
Wo kann ich ein Boot mieten?
voh kan ıсн īn boht mee'-tĕn?

Where can we fish for trout?
Wo können wir Forellen fischen?
voh kö'-nĕn veer fo'-rel-lĕn fish'-ĕn?

I need a gun for hunting.
Ich brauche ein Jagdgewehr.
ıсн brou'-khĕ īn yahgt'-gĕ-vehr.

Where can I buy ammunition?
Wo kann ich Munition kaufen?
voh kan ıсн moo'-ni-tsion kou'-fĕn?

What is the best place for hunting?
Wo jagd man am besten?
voh yahgt man am be'-stĕn?

What is the open season on deer?
Wann ist es erlaubt, auf Rotwild zu schiessen?
van ist es ĕr-loupt', ouf roht'-vilt tsoo shee'-sĕn?

The hunting season is from December to March.
Das Jagen ist von Dezember bis März erlaubt.
das yah'-gĕn ist fon deh-tsem'-bĕr bis merts er'-loupt'.

Skiing

How much do the ski lifts cost by the day?
Wieviel kostet der Skiaufzug (or: Skilift) pro Tag?
vee-feel' ko'-stĕt dehr shee'-ouf-tzook (or: shee'-lift) proh tahk?

Can I rent skis?
Kann ich mir Skier ausleihen?
kan icH meer shee'-er ous'-li-ĕn?

Other Sports

May I have 2 tickets, close to the ringside.
Kann ich zwei Sitzplätze dicht am Ring haben?
kan icH tsvi sits'-ple-tsĕ dicHt am ring hah'-bĕn?

How much will they cost?
Wieviel kosten sie?
vee-feel' ko'-stĕn zee?

Is it a championship fight?
Ist es ein Meisterschaftskampf?
ist es in mi'-stĕr-shafts-kampf?

How many days have the contestants been racing?
Seit wieviel Tagen kämpfen die Wettbewerber?
zit vee-feel' tah'-gĕn kem'-pfĕn dee vet'-bĕ-ver-bĕr?

How many kms. do they cover?
Wieviel Kilometer müssen sie zurücklegen?
vee-feel' ki'-loh-meh-ter mü'-sĕn zee tsoo-rük'-leh-gĕn?

What is the price range for tickets?
Wie hoch sind die Eintrittspreise?
vee hohkh zind dee in'-trits-pri-zĕ?

Where is the soccer field?
Wo ist der Fussballplatz?
voh ist dehr foos'-bal-plats?

CONDUCTING BUSINESS

I wish to apply for a visa.
Ich möchte ein Visum haben.
icH möcH'-tĕ in vee'-zum hah'-bĕn.

When will my visa be ready?
Wann kann ich mein Visum abholen?
van kan icH min vee'-zum ap'-hoh-lĕn?

Here is my identity card.
Hier ist meine Ausweiskarte.
heer ist mi'-nĕ ous'-wis-kar-tĕ.

For how long a period is my card valid?
Für wie lange ist meine Karte gültig?
führ wee lang'-ĕ ist mi'-nĕ kar-tĕ gül-ticH?

I would like to contact a firm that makes shoes.
**Ich möchte mich mit einer Firma in Verbindung setzen, die Schuhe
herstellt.**
*icH möcH'-tĕ micH mit ĭ'-nĕr fir'-mah in fer-bin'-dung zets'-ĕn, dee
shu-ĕ hehr'-shtelt.*

I am here to survey the market.
Ich bin hier, die Geschäftsverhältnisse zu prüfen.
icH bin heer, dee gĕ-shefts'-fĕr-helt-ni-sĕ tsoo prüh'-fĕn.

I need a local distributor for my product.
**Ich brauche einen hier ansässigen Vertreter meiner Ware
(or: Fabrikate).**
*icH brou'-khĕ ĭ'-nĕn heer an'-se-si-gĕn fĕr-treh'-tĕr mĭ'-nĕr
wah'-rĕ (or: fa-bri-kah'-tĕ).*

How can I check on a firm's credit rating?
Wie kann ich die finanzielle Lage einer Firma nachprüfen?
vee kan icH dee fi-nan-tsie'-lĕ lah'-gĕ ĭ'-nĕr fir'-mah nahkh'-prüh-fĕn?

May I show you these samples?
Darf ich Ihnen diese Proben zeigen?
darf icH ee'-nĕn dee'-zĕ proh'-bĕn tsĭ'-gĕn?

Can this product be manufactured here?
Kann diese Ware hier hergestellt werden?
kan dee'-zĕ vah'-rĕ heer hehr'-gĕ-shtelt vehr'-dĕn?

How large is your factory?
Wie gross ist Ihre Fabrik?
vee grohs ist ee'-rĕ fa-brik'?

How many people do you employ?
Wieviele Leute beschäftigen Sie?
vee-fee'-lĕ loi'-tĕ bĕ-shef'-ti-gĕn zee?

What is your capital?
Wie hoch ist (or: Wie hoch beläuft sich) Ihr Kapital?
vee hohkh ist (or: vee hohkh bĕ-loift' zicH) eer ka-pi-tahl?

I would like bank references.
Ich möchte Bankreferenzen haben.
icH möcH-tĕ bangk'-re-fĕ-rĕn-tsĕn hah'-bĕn.

I am authorized to pay for goods in dollars.
**Ich habe Vollmacht (or: Ich bin bevollmächtigt), die Ware in
Dollar zu bezahlen.**
*icH hah'-bĕ fol'-makht (or: icH bin bĕ-fol'-mecH-ticHt),
dee vah'-rĕ in do'-lahr tsoo bĕ-tsah'-lĕn.*

Where can you ship the merchandise (to)?
Wohin können Sie die Ware absenden (or: verschiffen)?
voh-hin' kö'-nĕn zee dee vah'-rĕ ap'-zen-dĕn (or: fĕr-shi'-fĕn)?

OUTLINE OF GERMAN GRAMMAR

Although, for purposes of everyday practical needs, you will be able to get by with some stock of common German words and phrases, it is advisable also to have some understanding of the parts of speech and their various forms as well as of the manner in which German sentences are constructed. In the following pages we have attempted to present the "highlights" of German grammar very concisely, so as to enable you to understand the how and why of the phrases in this book. This survey is of necessity brief, but the main facts for your daily needs have been covered.

THE ARTICLE

1.1. The definite article in German is declined for number, gender, and case:[1]

	Masculine	Feminine	Neuter	Plural of all three genders
Nominative	der	die	das	die
Genitive	des	der	des	der
Dative	dem	der	dem	den
Accusative	den	die	das	die

1.2. In German the gender is grammatical; even inanimate objects take a masculine, feminine, or neuter article. Therefore, every noun must be learned with its proper article.

Diminutives in *-chen* and *-lein* are neuter, regardless of their sex and the gender of the words from which they are derived. Examples: *die Frau* (the woman), *das Fräulein* (the young lady or miss); *der Hund* (the dog), *das Hündchen* (the little dog or puppy).

---

[1] German has four cases, the basic uses of which are: The *nominative* indicates the subject of the sentence. The *genitive* indicates possession and is usually translated by "of the" or the English possessive case like *der Hut des Vaters* (the father's hat). The *dative* is used for the indirect object of the verb and is usually translated by "to the" or "for the." The *accusative* is used for the direct object of the verb.

1.3. The forms of the indefinite article in German are:

	Masc.	*Fem.*	*Neuter*
Nom.	**ein**	**eine**	**ein**
Gen.	**eines**	**einer**	**eines**
Dat.	**einem**	**einer**	**einem**
Acc.	**einen**	**eine**	**ein**

1.4. Both the definite and indefinite articles agree in gender, number, and case with the noun they modify.

1.5. The inflection of adjectives and different types of pronouns follows to a considerable extent the declension of the definite article. The possessive adjectives and the negative *kein* (no) are declined as the indefinite article.

THE NOUN

2.0. There are three declensions in German:

2.1. Nouns that have different endings in the plural and whose stem vowel is often modified by an umlaut belong to the so-called strong declension:

Singular

Nom.	**der Vater** (father)	**die Hand** (hand)	**das Jahr** (year)
Gen.	**des Vaters**	**der Hand**	**des Jahr(e)s**
Dat.	**dem Vater**	**der Hand**	**dem Jahr**
Acc.	**den Vater**	**die Hand**	**das Jahr**

Plural

Nom.	**die Väter**	**die Hände**	**die Jahre**
Gen.	**der Väter**	**der Hände**	**der Jahre**
Dat.	**den Vätern**	**den Händen**	**den Jahren**
Acc.	**die Väter**	**die Hände**	**die Jahre**

2.2. Nouns the stem vowel of which is not modified and which form the plural by adding -*(e)n* to the nominative singular belong to the so-called weak declension:

Singular: **die, der, der, die *Frau*;** Plural: **die, der, den, die *Frauen*.**

Although the weak declension is fundamentally a declension of feminine nouns, it contains a certain number of masculine nouns which take an -*(e)n* in both the singular and the plural except in the nominative singular; e.g. *der Knabe* (the boy), *des Knaben* (of the boy) and other masculine nouns ending in -*e* denoting masculine beings.

2.3. A number of nouns that have a genitive in -*s* and form their plural in -*(e)n* belong to the so-called mixed declension which is a combination of the other two declensions:

	Singular		Plural	
Nom.	der Schmerz (pain)	das Auge (eye)	die Schmerzen	die Augen
Gen.	des Schmerzes	des Auges	der Schmerzen	der Augen
Dat.	dem Schmerz	dem Auge	den Schmerzen	den Augen
Acc.	den Schmerz	das Auge	die Schmerzen	die Augen

2.4. Proper names are usually not declined in German with the exception that they generally take an ending in the genitive.

2.5. German has a great number of compound nouns; e.g. *das Schlafzimmer* (*der Schlaf* [the sleep] + *das Zimmer* [the room]), the bedroom: *der Badezimmerschlüssel* (*das Bad* [the bath] + *das Zimmer* [the room] + *der Schlüssel* [the key]), the bathroom key.

THE ADJECTIVE

3.0. There are three declensions of adjectives in German: strong, weak, and mixed:

3.1. The Strong Adjective Declension.

Singular

	Masculine	Feminine	Neuter
Nom.	guter Vater (good father)	gute Mutter (good mother)	gutes Kind (good child)
Gen.	guten Vaters	guter Mutter	guten Kind(e)s
Dat.	gutem Vater	guter Mutter	gutem Kind(e)
Acc.	guten Vater	gute Mutter	gutes Kind

Plural

	Masculine	Feminine	Neuter
Nom.	gute Mütter	gute Väter	gute Kinder
Gen.	guter Mütter	guter Väter	guter Kinder
Dat.	guten Müttern	guten Vätern	guten Kindern
Acc.	gute Mütter	gute Väter	gute Kinder

3.2. The Weak Adjective Declension.

Singular

	Masculine	Feminine	Neuter
Nom.	der gute Vater	die gute Mutter	das gute Kind
Gen.	des guten Vaters	der guten Mutter	des guten Kind(e)s
Dat.	dem guten Vater	der guten Mutter	dem guten Kind
Acc.	den guten Vater	die gute Mutter	das gute Kind

Plural

Nom.	die guten Väter	die guten Mütter	die guten Kinder
Gen.	der guten Väter	der guten Mütter	der guten Kinder
Dat.	den guten Vätern	den guten Müttern	den guten Kindern
Acc.	die guten Väter	die guten Mütter	die guten Kinder

3.3. The Mixed Adjective Declension.

Singular

	Masculine	*Feminine*	*Neuter*
Nom.	ein guter Vater	eine gute Mutter	ein gutes Kind
Gen.	eines guten Vaters	einer guten Mutter	eines guten Kind(e)s
Dat.	einem guten Vater	einer guten Mutter	einem guten Kind
Acc.	einen guten Vater	eine gute Mutter	ein gutes Kind

Plural

keine guten Väter	**keine** guten Mütter	**keine** guten Kinder
keiner guten Väter	**keiner** guten Mütter	**keiner** guten Kinder
keinen guten Vätern	**keinen** guten Müttern	**keinen** guten Kindern
keine guten Väter	**keine** guten Mütter	**keine** guten Kinder

Note that in the strong declension all cases in the singular and the plural, except those of the genitives of the masculine and neuter singular, are declined as the definite article.

Note that in the weak declension all cases, except the three nominative singulars and the accusative singulars of the feminine and neuter, have the ending *-en*.

The weak adjective declension is used whenever the adjective is preceded by one of the *der*-forms. When it is preceded by an *ein*-word, it is declined as the weak declension but there are three cases where it takes strong endings. (They are: nom. sing. masculine and nom. and acc. sing. neuter.)

3.4. The adjective agrees in gender, number, and case with the noun it modifies.

3.5. Adjectives in German are not declined after the verbs *sein* (to be), *werden* (to become, get), and some others and when they are used as an adverb: *Gertrud schreibt und liest gut* (Gertrude writes and reads well).

3.6. The adjectives in German, as in English, may be used as nouns: *der Alte* (the old man), *die Grosse* (the tall one).

3.7. The comparative in German is formed by adding *-er* and the superlative by adding *-(e)st* to the basic form of the adjective as in English: *klein* (small), *kleiner* (smaller), *kleinster* (smallest).

In the comparative and superlative, monosyllabic adjectives usually take an umlaut (*a, o, u* change to *ä, ö, ü*). There are two forms of the superlative in German: (1) The form given above and (2) a form in *am -(e)sten* after the verbs *sein* and *werden: Im Juni sind die Tage am längsten* (In June the days are longest).

3.8. Five adjectives have irregular comparative and superlative forms:

Positive	Comparative	Superlative
gut good	**besser** better	**best** best
gross large	**grösser** larger	**grösst** largest
hoch high	**höher** higher	**höchst** highest
nah near	**näher** nearer	**nächst** nearest
viel much	**mehr** more	**meist** most

3.9. The comparison of equality in German is expressed by *so ... wie* (as ... as): *Georg ist so gut wie Karl* (George is as good as Charles).

The comparison of inequality in German is expressed by the comparative of the adjective followed by *als: Georg ist ärmer als Johann* (George is poorer than John).

THE PRONOUN

4.1. The personal pronouns are:

Singular

	1st Person	2nd Person	3rd Person Masc.	Fem.	Neut.
Nom.	**ich** (I)	**du** (you)	**er** (he)	**sie** (she)	**es** (it)
Gen.	**meiner** (of me)	**deiner**	**seiner**	**ihrer**	**seiner**
Dat.	**mir** (to me)	**dir**	**ihm**	**ihr**	**ihm**
Acc.	**mich** (me)	**dich**	**ihn**	**sie**	**es**

Plural

				Polite Form
Nom.	**wir** (we)	**ihr** (you)	**sie** (they)	**Sie** (you)
Gen.	**unser** (of us)	**euer** (of you)	**ihrer** (of them)	**Ihrer** (of you)
Dat.	**uns** (to us)	**euch** (to you)	**ihnen** (to them)	**Ihnen** (to you)
Acc.	**uns** (us)	**euch** (you)	**sie** (they)	**Sie** (you)

The forms of the genitive case are rarely used in modern German.

4.1.a. Note that "you" can be translated in three ways in German:

a. The *du*-form, which is used in addressing the Deity, close friends, relatives, children and pets.

b. The plural of *du* is *ihr* and is used as the familiar plural form.

c. Sie is used in addressing mere acquaintances or strangers, whether singular or plural. It has the same form as the third person plural, and to distinguish it from this form it is written with a capital letter.

4.1.b. Whenever a personal pronoun referring to an object or idea is used in English after a preposition, e.g. "of it," "with it," etc., *da* is used in German instead of the proper pronoun and the preposition is compounded with the particle: *davon, damit,* etc. These pronominal compounds never refer to people. If the preposition begins with a vowel, an *r* is inserted between *da* and the preposition: *da + r + an = daran* (at it, on it, etc.).

4.2. The reflexive pronouns of the first and second persons, singular and plural, have no special form, but generally use the forms of the accusative of the personal pronoun; only the third person and the polite form of "you" have the special reflexive form *sich* for all of them. Verbs are used reflexively in German more often than in English: *Ich freue mich* (I am glad); *setzen Sie sich* (sit down).

4.3. The possessive adjectives and pronouns are:

Singular

	Masculine	*Feminine*	*Neuter*
1st person	**mein** (my)	**meine**	**mein**
2nd person	**dein** (your)	**deine**	**dein**
3rd person (masc.)	**sein** (his)	**seine**	**sein**
3rd person (fem.)	**ihr** (her, your p.s.)	**ihre**	**ihr**

Plural

1st person	**unser** (our)	**uns(e)re**	**unser**
2nd person	**euer** (your)	**eu(e)re**	**euer**
3rd person	**ihr** (their, your p.f.)	**ihre**	**ihr**

They are inflected as *ein*-words except in the singular masculine nominative and singular neuter nominative and accusative. In these cases they take an ending when the possessive adjective is used as a pronoun.

4.4. The most common **demonstrative adjectives and pronouns** in German are *dieser* (this one) and *jener* (that one). They are declined as the definite article. Definite articles are also used as demonstrative pronouns: *Hat Fritz es getan? Nein,* **der** *hat es nicht getan.* (Did Fred do it? No, *he* did not do it.)

There are two demonstrative compound pronouns: *derselbe* (the same), made up of the definite article *der* and *selbe* (same), and *derjenige* (he who). They are rarely used.

4.5. The **interrogative pronouns** are:

	Masculine and Feminine	*Neuter*
Nom.	**wer** (who)	**was** (what)
Gen.	**wessen** (whose)	—
Dat.	**wem** (to whom, etc.)	—
Acc.	**wen** (whom)	**was** (what)

Questions expressed in English by "what" and a preposition, such as "of what," "with what," "on what," etc., are translated into German by *wovon, womit, worauf*, etc. In each case the interrogative *wo* is used with the required preposition.

There is also the interrogative expression *was für* (what kind of), which has no prepositional force and does not affect *ein* or the following noun. Where more than one object or person is referred to, *ein* is dropped: *Was für ein Mädchen ist sie?* (What kind of a girl is she?); *was für Bücher haben Sie da?* (what kind of books do you have there?).

4.6. The declension of the **relative pronouns** in German is very similar to the definite article:

	Masculine	*Feminine*	*Neuter*	*Plural*
Nom.	**der** (who)	**die** (who)	**das** (that, which)	**die** (who, which)
Gen.	**dessen** (whose)	**deren** (whose)	**dessen** (of which)	**deren** (whose, of which)
Dat.	**dem** (to whom)	**der** (to whom)	**dem** (to which)	**denen** (to whom, to which)
Acc.	**den** (whom)	**die** (whom)	**das** (that, which)	**die** (whom, which)

The relative pronouns agree in gender and number with the noun of the main clause to which they refer but their case is determined by their function in the relative clause: *das ist die Frau, der ich das Geld gab* (that is the woman to whom I gave the money); *das ist die Frau, die mir das Geld gab* (that is the woman who gave me the money).

There is another relative pronoun *welch* (which), not so commonly used as the form based on the article.

When relative pronouns refer to an unknown or indefinite antecedent, they have the same form as interrogative pronouns.

4.7. There are three classes of **indefinite pronouns:**

a. Pronouns that are not declined:

1) *man* (one, they, or people), used only in the singular as subject of a verb; *man spricht Englisch* (they, we speak English). Constructions with *man* can often best be rendered by a passive form in English, in this case "English is spoken."

2) *etwas* (something) and *nichts* (nothing) are used as subject, object.

b. Pronouns that are inflected only in the genitive case: *jemand* (someone, somebody); *niemand* (no one, nobody); and *jedermann* (everybody, everyone).

c. Pronouns that are declined as the definite article: *einer* (one), *keiner* (none, nobody), *jeder* (each one), *beide* (both), *wenig* (little), *wenige* (few, a few), *viel* (much), *viele* (many), *all* (all).

THE PREPOSITION

5.1. In German, prepositions are followed by the accusative, dative, or genitive case, and they may be grouped according to the case they require, as follows:

a. Prepositions that require the **accusative:** *bis* (to, till), *durch* (through), *für* (for), *gegen* (against), *ohne* (without), *um* (around, at) and *wider* (against).

b. Prepositions that require the **dative:** *aus* (out of, from), *ausser* (except, beside), *bei* (at, near, at the house of), *mit* (with), *nach* (after, to), *seit* (since, in expressions of time), *von* (from, of, by), *zu* (to).

c. Prepositions that require the **genitive:** *anstatt, statt* (instead of), *trotz* (in spite of), *während* (during), *wegen* (because of).

d. Prepositions that take either the **dative** or **accusative:** *an* (at, to, up to [an object]), *auf* (on, upon, on top of), *hinter* (behind, in back of), *in* (in, into), *neben* (beside, next to), *über* (over, above), *unter* (under; among), *vor* (before, in front of, ago), *zwischen* (between).

Note. The dative case follows these prepositions when they indicate the place where an object is or an action takes place, and the accusative when they imply motion to a place.

5.2. The use of the prepositions is largely idiomatic. One should form the habit of observing and learning, through repetition and practice, the prepositional usages which differ from English as one encounters them.

5.3. Some prepositions contract with the definite article in the dative or accusative case: *an dem* → **am**; *an das* → **ans**; *in dem* → **im**; *in das* → **ins**; *von dem* → **vom**; *zu dem* → **zum**; *zu der* → **zur**; *auf das* → **aufs**.

THE CONJUNCTION

6.1. Coordinating conjunctions join sentences, clauses, phrases, and words of equal rank. The most common ones are: *aber* (but), *oder* (or), *sondern* (but [on the contrary]), *und* (and), *entweder . . . oder* (either . . . or), *weder . . . noch* (neither . . . nor).

6.2. Subordinating conjunctions introduce dependent clauses. The most common ones are: *als* (when, than, as), *als ob* (as if), *bevor* (before), *falls* (in case), *indem* (while), *je . . . desto* (the . . . the), *nachdem* (after), *ob* (whether), *obgleich, obschon* (although), *seitdem* (since [time]), *wann* (when), *weil* (because), *wenn* (when, if) *wenn auch* (though), *während* (while), *wie* (how, as), *wo* (where).

WORD ORDER

6.3. After coordinating conjunctions, which connect two principal or main clauses, the so-called normal word order does not change. The subject comes first, the verb follows. (See also 7.5.)

6.4. The dependent clause requires a special word order in German. In simple tenses, the verb proper is at the end of the subordinate clause. In compound tenses, the inflected part comes last and the past participle or infinitive precedes it: *die Wörter, die du gelernt hast, werden dir sehr nützlich sein* (the words you learned will be very useful to you).

THE ADVERB

7.1. In German adverbs have no special endings. Almost any adjective can be used as an adverb without any change in its form. Their comparative and superlative forms are also formed exactly as those of the corresponding adjectives.

7.2. There are a few adverbs which can never be used as adjectives, such as *sehr* (very), *gern* (like), *bald* (soon).

7.3. The comparative and superlative of *gern* are: *lieber, liebst* or *am liebsten*, and of *bald: eher* or *früher, ehest* or *frühst* or *am ehesten* or *am frühsten*.

7.4. Sometimes independent adverbs are formed from adjectives by adding *-weise* (from *die Weise* [the manner, way]) to the adjective: *glücklicherweise* (fortunately).

7.5. When a sentence begins with an adverb or an adverbial phrase, the word order is inverted; that is, the verb comes before the subject noun.

THE VERB

8.1. The irregular auxiliary verbs *sein* (to be), *haben* (to have) and *werden* (to become) are used in the formation of the compound tenses of the other verbs.

INDICATIVE

Present

ich bin *(I am)*	ich habe *(I have)*	ich werde *(I become)*
du bist	du hast	du wirst
er, sie, es ist	er, sie, es hat	er, sie, es wird
wir sind	wir haben	wir werden
ihr seid	ihr habt	ihr werdet
sie, Sie sind	sie, Sie haben	sie, Sie werden

Past

ich war *(I was)*	ich hatte *(I had)*	ich wurde *(I became)*
du warst	du hattest	du wurdest
er war	er hatte	er wurde
wir waren	wir hatten	wir wurden
ihr wart	ihr hattet	ihr wurdet
sie, Sie waren	sie, Sie hatten	sie, Sie wurden

In German the present and the past correspond to three different possible forms in English, e.g. *ich habe* can mean "I have," "I am having" and "I do have," and *ich hatte* can stand for "I had," "I was having" and "I did have."

Perfect

ich bin gewesen	ich habe gehabt	ich bin geworden
(I have been)	*(I have had)*	*(I have become)*
du bist gewesen	du hast gehabt	du bist geworden
etc.	*etc.*	*etc.*

Pluperfect

ich war gewesen	ich hatte gehabt	ich war geworden
(I had been)	*(I had had)*	*(I had become)*
du warst gewesen	du hattest gehabt	du warst geworden
etc.	*etc.*	*etc.*

Future

ich werde sein	ich werde haben	ich werde werden
(I shall be)	*(I shall have)*	*(I shall become)*
du wirst sein	du wirst haben	du wirst werden
etc.	*etc.*	*etc.*

Future Perfect

ich werde gewesen sein	werde gehabt haben	werde geworden sein
(I shall have been)	*(shall have had)*	*(shall have become)*
etc.	*etc.*	*etc.*

The perfect is formed by the present of *haben* or *sein* plus the past participle; the pluperfect by the past of *haben* or *sein* and the past participle of the verb.

Haben is used with practically all verbs, *sein* being used only with intransitive verbs showing a change of place or condition: *Er* **hat** *eine Reise* **gemacht** (He *made (has made)* a trip); *Sie* **hatte** *den Brief* **gelesen** (She *had read* the letter); *Er* **ist** *in den Park* **gegangen** (He *went (has gone)* to the park); *Wir* **sind** *spät* **eingeschlafen** (We *fell (have fallen)* asleep late).

The future is formed by the present of *werden* with the infinitive of the verb, and the future perfect by the present of *werden,* the past participle of the verb and the infinitive of *haben* or *sein.*

8.2. There are two conjugations of verbs in German: the weak and the strong conjugations.

German *weak* verbs correspond very closely to English regular verbs: *folgen* (to follow), *folgte* (followed), *gefolgt* (followed).

German *strong* verbs correspond to the English irregular verbs: *springen* (to spring), *sprang* (sprang), *gesprungen* (sprung).

The most outstanding characteristic of the German strong and the English irregular verbs is the change of the stem vowel in the different tenses. The weak and the strong verbs have these features in common.

All infinitives in German have the ending *-en: gehen* (to go) or *-n: tun* (to do) added to the stem of the verb. From this stem all the tenses of the weak verbs are formed, but only the present of the strong verbs.

The endings of the present tense are the same, whether the verb is weak or strong.

INDICATIVE

Present

Weak Conjugation	*Strong Conjugation*	*Reflexive Verb*
ich mache	ich lese	ich freue mich
(I make)	*(I read)*	*(I am glad)*
du machst	du liest	du freust dich
er macht	er liest	er freut sich
wir machen	wir lesen	wir freuen uns
ihr macht	ihr lest	ihr freut euch
sie machen	sie lesen	sie freuen sich

Past

ich machte	ich las	ich freute mich
du machtest	du last	du freutest dich
er machte	er las	er freute sich
wir machten	wir lasen	wir freuten uns
ihr machtet	ihr last	ihr freutet euch
sie machten	sie lasen	sie freuten sich

Perfect

ich habe gemacht	ich habe gelesen	ich habe mich gefreut
du hast gemacht	du hast gelesen	du hast dich gefreut
etc.	*etc.*	*etc.*

Pluperfect

ich hatte gemacht	ich hatte gelesen	ich hatte mich gefreut
du hattest gemacht	du hattest gelesen	du hattest dich gefreut
etc.	*etc.*	*etc.*

Future

ich werde machen	ich werde lesen	ich werde mich freuen
du wirst machen	du wirst lesen	du wirst dich freuen
etc.	*etc.*	*etc.*

Future Perfect

ich werde gemacht haben *etc.*	. . . gelesen haben *etc.*	. . . mich gefreut haben *etc.*

8.3. The subjunctive may be used in indirect discourse, especially when the verb of the main clause is not in the present. It is also used in unreal conditions and in expressing wishes, polite requests, doubts, necessities, etc., and after *als ob* (as if).

SUBJUNCTIVE

Present

ich mache	ich lese	ich freue mich
du machest	du lesest	du freuest dich
er mache	er lese	er freue sich
wir machen	wir lesen	wir freuen uns
ihr machet	ihr leset	ihr freuet euch
sie machen	sie lesen	sie freuen sich

Past

ich machte	ich läse	ich freute mich
du machtest	du läsest	du freutest dich
er machte	er läse	er freute sich
wir machten	wir läsen	wir freuten uns
ihr machtet	ihr läset	ihr freutet euch
sie machten	sie läsen	sie freuten sich

8.4. The conditional is used, as the subjunctive, in expressing unreal conditions. The conditional is preferred with strong verbs, and the subjunctive is used more commonly with weak verbs. In addition to its use in contrary-to-fact statements, the conditional can be used to soften requests or make them more polite, such as *würden Sie das tun?* (would you please do that?) rather than *wollen Sie das tun?* (do you want to do that?).

Conditional

ich würde machen	ich würde lesen	ich würde mich freuen
etc.	*etc.*	*etc.*

Conditional Perfect

ich würde gemacht haben	. . . gelesen haben	. . . mich gefreut haben
etc.	*etc.*	*etc.*

8.5. The imperative has one form for the familiar singular, one form for the familiar plural, and one form for both the singular and plural in polite address.

Imperative

mache	lies	freue dich
macht	lest	freut euch
machen Sie	lesen Sie	freuen Sie sich

VERB LIST

8.6. The verb list is composed of two sections: strong (irregular) verbs and modal auxiliary verbs.

Weak verbs are not included because all tenses and forms of the weak verb can be derived from the stem of the infinitive by attaching the regular endings to it.

The *principal parts,* that is to say, the infinitive, third person singular of the present indicative and past indicative, past participle, and the irregularly formed imperative, familiar form, are given. From these given forms, all other forms and tenses can be derived by the addition of the appropriate endings to the required stem.

The verb forms are given in the *third person singular* because this form shows any irregularity in the present and gives the past stem.

If the past participle is preceded by *ist* (third person sing. of *sein*), the compound tenses of the verb are conjugated with the appropriate form of *sein.* If the past participle alone is given, the compound tenses are conjugated with the appropriate form of *haben.*

The imperative is given in the singular familiar form only when the vowel of the infinitive stem changes from *e* to *i* in the imperative. All other imperatives are regularly formed from the infinitive. Some verbs do not have imperatives because of the nature of their meaning, i.e., modal auxiliaries have no imperatives because, obviously, an order cannot be formulated upon them.

Many new verbs can be formed by the addition of a prefix to a basic verb. These compounds follow the conjugation of the original verb and, therefore, are not listed here.

STRONG VERBS

INFINITIVE	PRESENT INDICATIVE	PAST INDICATIVE	PAST PARTICIPLE	IMPERATIVE
backen (to bake)	**bäckt**	**buk**	**gebacken**	
befehlen (to command)	**befiehlt**	**befahl**	**befohlen**	**befiehl**
beginnen (to begin)	**beginnt**	**begann**	**begonnen**	

79

INFINITIVE	PRESENT INDICATIVE	PAST INDICATIVE	PAST PARTICIPLE	IMPERATIVE
beissen (to bite)	beisst	biss	gebissen	
bergen (to conceal)	birgt	barg	geborgen	birg
bersten (to burst)	birst	barst	(ist) geborsten	birst
betrügen (to deceive)	betrügt	betrog	betrogen	
bewegen (to induce)	bewegt	bewog	bewogen	
biegen (to bend)	biegt	bog	gebogen	
bieten (to offer)	bietet	bot	geboten	
binden (to bind)	bindet	band	gebunden	
bitten (to beg, to ask)	bittet	bat	gebeten	
blasen (to blow)	bläst	blies	geblasen	
bleiben (to remain)	bleibt	blieb	(ist) geblieben	
braten (to roast)	brät	briet	gebraten	
brechen (to break)	bricht	brach	gebrochen	brich
dringen (to press)	dringt	drang	(ist) gedrungen	
einladen (to invite)	lädt ein	lud ein	eingeladen	
empfehlen (to recommend)	empfiehlt	empfahl	empfohlen	empfiehl
erbleichen (to turn pale)	erbleicht	erblich	(ist) erblichen	
erlöschen (to extinguish, to go out)	erlischt	erlosch	(ist) erloschen	erlisch
erschrecken (to be frightened)	erschrickt	erschrak	(ist) erschrocken	erschrick
essen (to eat)	isst	ass	gegessen	iss
fahren (to drive, ride)	fährt	fuhr	(ist) gefahren	
fallen (to fall)	fällt	fiel	(ist) gefallen	

Infinitive	Present Indicative	Past Indicative	Past Participle	Imperative
fangen (to catch)	**fängt**	**fing**	**gefangen**	
fechten (to fence)	**ficht**	**focht**	**gefochten**	**ficht**
finden (to find)	**findet**	**fand**	**gefunden**	
flechten (to braid)	**flicht**	**flocht**	**geflochten**	**flicht**
fliegen (to fly)	**fliegt**	**flog**	(ist) **geflogen**	
fliehen (to flee)	**flieht**	**floh**	(ist) **geflohen**	
fliessen (to flow)	**fliesst**	**floss**	(ist) **geflossen**	
fressen (to eat [of animals])	**frisst**	**frass**	**gefressen**	**friss**
frieren (to freeze)	**friert**	**fror**	**gefroren**	
gebären (to bear, give birth)	**gebiert**	**gebar**	**geboren**	**gebier**
geben (to give)	**gibt**	**gab**	**gegeben**	**gib**
gedeihen (to thrive)	**gedeiht**	**gedieh**	(ist) **gediehen**	
gehen (to go)	**geht**	**ging**	(ist) **gegangen**	
gelingen (to succeed)	**gelingt**	**gelang**	(ist) **gelungen**	
gelten (to be worth)	**gilt**	**galt**	**gegolten**	
genesen (to recover)	**genest**	**genas**	(ist) **genesen**	
geniessen (to enjoy)	**geniesst**	**genoss**	**genossen**	
geschehen (to happen)	**geschieht**	**geschah**	(ist) **geschehen**	
gewinnen (to gain, to get)	**gewinnt**	**gewann**	**gewonnen**	
giessen (to pour)	**giesst**	**goss**	**gegossen**	
gleichen (to resemble)	**gleicht**	**glich**	**geglichen**	
gleiten (to glide)	**gleitet**	**glitt**	(ist) **geglitten**	

Infinitive	Present Indicative	Past Indicative	Past Participle	Imperative
glimmen (to gleam)	**glimmt**	**glomm**	**geglommen**	
graben (to dig)	**gräbt**	**grub**	**gegraben**	
greifen (to seize)	**greift**	**griff**	**gegriffen**	
halten (to hold)	**hält**	**hielt**	**gehalten**	
hängen (to hang, to be suspended)	**hängt**	**hing**	**gehangen**	
hauen (to hew, to strike)	**haut**	**hieb**	**gehauen**	
heben (to lift)	**hebt**	**hob**	**gehoben**	
heissen (to bid, to be called)	**heisst**	**hiess**	**geheissen**	
helfen (to help)	**hilft**	**half**	**geholfen**	**hilf**
klingen (to sound)	**klingt**	**klang**	**geklungen**	
kommen (to come)	**kommt**	**kam**	(ist) **gekommen**	
kriechen (to creep)	**kriecht**	**kroch**	(ist) **gekrochen**	
laden (to load)	**lädt or ladet**	**lud**	**geladen**	
lassen (to let)	**lässt**	**liess**	**gelassen**	
laufen (to run)	**läuft**	**lief**	(ist) **gelaufen**	
leiden (to suffer)	**leidet**	**litt**	**gelitten**	
leihen (to lend)	**leiht**	**lieh**	**geliehen**	
lesen (to read)	**liest**	**las**	**gelesen**	**lies**
liegen (to lie)	**liegt**	**lag**	**gelegen**	
lügen (to tell a lie)	**lügt**	**log**	**gelogen**	
meiden (to avoid)	**meidet**	**mied**	**gemieden**	
messen (to measure)	**misst**	**mass**	**gemessen**	**miss**

INFINITIVE	PRESENT INDICATIVE	PAST INDICATIVE	PAST PARTICIPLE	IMPERATIVE
misslingen (to fail)	misslingt	misslang	(ist) misslungen	
nehmen (to take)	nimmt	nahm	genommen	nimm
pfeifen (to whistle)	pfeift	pfiff	gepfiffen	
preisen (to praise)	preist	pries	gepriesen	
quellen (to gush, to well)	quillt	quoll	(ist) gequollen	quill
raten (to advise)	rät	riet	geraten	
reiben (to rub)	reibt	rieb	gerieben	
reissen (to tear)	reisst	riss	gerissen	
reiten (to ride)	reitet	ritt	(ist) geritten	
riechen (to smell)	riecht	roch	gerochen	
rufen (to call)	ruft	rief	gerufen	
saufen (to drink [of animals])	säuft	soff	gesoffen	
schaffen (to create)	schafft	schuf	geschaffen	
schallen (to sound)	schallt	scholl	geschollen	
scheiden (to part)	scheidet	schied	(ist) geschieden	
scheinen (to appear, to shine)	scheint	schien	geschienen	
schelten (to scold)	schilt	schalt	gescholten	schilt
schieben (to shove, to push)	schiebt	schob	geschoben	
schiessen (to shoot)	schiesst	schoss	geschossen	
schlafen (to sleep)	schläft	schlief	geschlafen	
schlagen (to strike)	schlägt	schlug	geschlagen	
schleichen (to sneak)	schleicht	schlich	(ist) geschlichen	

INFINITIVE	PRESENT INDICATIVE	PAST INDICATIVE	PAST PARTICIPLE	IMPERATIVE
schleifen (to whet, to grind)	schleift	schliff	geschliffen	
schliessen (to shut)	schliesst	schloss	geschlossen	
schmelzen (to melt)	schmilzt	schmolz	(ist) geschmolzen	schmilz
schneiden (to cut)	schneidet	schnitt	geschnitten	
schrauben (to screw)	schraubt	schrob	geschroben	
schreiben (to write)	schreibt	schrieb	geschrieben	
schreien (to cry out, to shout)	schreit	schrie	geschrieen	
schreiten (to stride)	schreitet	schritt	(ist) geschritten	
schweigen (to be silent)	schweigt	schwieg	geschwiegen	
schwellen (to swell)	schwillt	schwoll	(ist) geschwollen	schwill
schwimmen (to swim)	schwimmt	schwamm	(ist) geschwommen	
schwinden (to vanish)	schwindet	schwand	(ist) geschwunden	
schwingen (to swing)	schwingt	schwang	geschwungen	
schwören (to swear)	schwört	schwor, schwur	geschworen	
sehen (to see)	sieht	sah	gesehen	sieh
sieden (to simmer, to seethe)	siedet	sott	gesotten	
singen (to sing)	singt	sang	gesungen	
sinken (to sink)	sinkt	sank	(ist) gesunken	
sinnen (to think, to reflect)	sinnt	sann	gesonnen	
sitzen (to sit)	sitzt	sass	gesessen	
speien (to spit)	speit	spie	gespieen	
spinnen (to spin)	spinnt	spann	gesponnen	

INFINITIVE	PRESENT INDICATIVE	PAST INDICATIVE	PAST PARTICIPLE	IMPERATIVE
sprechen (to speak)	spricht	sprach	gesprochen	sprich
spriessen (to sprout)	spriesst	spross	(ist) gesprossen	
springen (to spring)	springt	sprang	(ist) gesprungen	
stechen (to prick)	sticht	stach	gestochen	stich
stehen (to stand)	steht	stand	gestanden	
stehlen (to steal)	stiehlt	stahl	gestohlen	stiehl
steigen (to ascend)	steigt	stieg	(ist) gestiegen	
sterben (to die)	stirbt	starb	(ist) gestorben	stirb
stossen (to push, to kick)	stösst	stiess	gestossen	
streichen (to stroke)	streicht	strich	gestrichen	
streiten (to argue)	streitet	stritt	gestritten	
tragen (to carry)	trägt	trug	getragen	
treffen (to hit, to meet)	trifft	traf	getroffen	triff
treiben (to drive)	treibt	trieb	getrieben	
treten (to step)	tritt	trat	(ist) getreten	tritt
trinken (to drink)	trinkt	trank	getrunken	
tun (to do)	tut	tat	getan	
verderben (to spoil)	verdirbt	verdarb	verdorben	verdirb
vergessen (to forget)	vergisst	vergass	vergessen	vergiss
verlieren (to lose)	verliert	verlor	verloren	
verzeihen (to pardon)	verzeiht	verzieh	verziehen	
wachsen (to grow)	wächst	wuchs	(ist) gewachsen	

INFINITIVE	PRESENT INDICATIVE	PAST INDICATIVE	PAST PARTICIPLE	IMPERATIVE
waschen (to wash)	wäscht	wusch	gewaschen	
weben (to weave)	webt	wob	gewoben	
weichen (to yield)	weicht	wich	(ist) gewichen	
weisen (to show)	weist	wies	gewiesen	
werben (to woo)	wirbt	warb	geworben	wirb
werfen (to throw)	wirft	warf	geworfen	wirf
wiegen (to weigh)	wiegt	wog	gewogen	
winden (to wind)	windet	wand	gewunden	
ziehen (to draw, to pull)	zieht	zog	gezogen	
zwingen (to force)	zwingt	zwang	gezwungen	

MODAL AUXILIARIES AND "WISSEN"

dürfen (to be allowed)	darf	durfte	gedurft	
können (can, to be able)	kann	konnte	gekonnt	
mögen (may, to like)	mag	mochte	gemocht	
müssen (must, to be compelled, have to)	muss	musste	gemusst	
sollen (shall, to be to, be said to)	soll	sollte	gesollt	
wollen (will, to want)	will	wollte	gewollt	
wissen (to know)	weiss	wusste	gewusst	

German-English Dictionary*

A

Abend,-e *m.* evening
Abendmahl,-e *n.* supper
aber but
abfahren *st.v.* to start, to depart
Abfahrt,-en *f.* departure
abholen to call for; to go to meet
abnützen to wear out
Absatz,-ˬe *m.* heel
abschütteln to shake off
abspielen *refl.* to proceed; to take place
absteigen *st.v.* to check in
Abteil,-e *n.* compartment
Abteilung,-en *f.* department
Abwesenheit,-en *f.* absence
abziehen *st.v.* to subtract, take off
Abzug,-ˬe *m.* deduction, discount
addieren to add
Adler,- *m.* eagle
Adresse,-n *f.* address
ähnlich similar
Ahnung,-en *f.* premonition
Aktentasche,-n *f.* brief case
all, alle all
Allee,-n *f.* avenue
allein alone
allerlei all kinds of things
allerseits to all
alles everything

allgemein general
  in allgemeinen in general
allmählich gradually
Alpen *pl.* Alps
als than, when
alt old
Alter,- *n.* age
Altertum,-ˬer *n.* antiquity
Amerika *n.* America
Amerikaner,- *m.* American (the)
amerikanisch *adj.* American
amüsieren *refl.* to have a good time
an at, to, on
ander other
anderes different
anderthalb (eineinhalb) one and a half
anbieten *st.v.* to offer
Anblick,-e *m.* view, sight
anerkennen to recognize
Anfang,-ˬe *m.* beginning
anfangen *st.v.* to begin
angebrochen opened, started
Angelegenheit,-en *f.* affair, matter
angenehm pleasant, pleased
angezogen werden *st.v.* to be attracted
Angst,-ˬe *f.* fear
Ankunft,-ˬe *f.* arrival
anlangen to arrive
anlegen to construct

---

*In the German-English and English-German dictionaries that follow, these points should be noted: Strong verbs are indicated by *st. v.*; irregular verbs, by *irr. v.*; irregular weak verbs, by *irr. w.v.*; reflexive verbs, by *refl.* For nouns, plurals are shown by endings added to the stem, and vowel changes, where necessary, are indicated by an umlaut preceding the ending (e.g., *Haus,-ˬer*). The genitive case is indicated only in the case of mixed declension nouns and irregularly declined nouns.

annehmen *st.v.* to accept, assume
anregen to stimulate
Anregung,-en *f.* stimulation
anrufen *st.v.* to call up, telephone
anschliessen *refl. st. v.* to join
ansehen *refl. st. v.* to look at
anstatt instead of
anstimmen to begin to sing
anstrengend strenuous
anvertrauen *refl.* to entrust oneself
  to
anziehen *st.v.* to dress, to tighten
  (screw)
  sich . . . to get dressed
Anzug,-¨e *m.* suit
Apfel,-¨ *m.* apple
Apfelmus *n.* applesauce
Apotheke,-n *f.* apothecary,
  drugstore
Apparat,-e *m.* apparatus
April *m.* April
Arbeit,-en *f.* work
arbeiten to work
arm poor
Arme,-e *m.* arm
Armbanduhr,-en *f.* wristwatch
Ärmel,- *m.* sleeve
Art,-en *f.* type, kind
Artikel,- *m.* article, commodity
Arzt,-¨e *m.* physician
atmen to breathe
auch also, too
auf on, upon, to
auf Wiedersehen good-bye, au revoir
aufbauen to build up
aufbewahren to store, check
  zum Aufbewahren for checking
  (baggage)
auffüllen to fill up
aufführen to perform
Aufführung,-en *f.* performance
aufgeregt excited
aufgewühlt sein to be wrought up
aufhängen *st.v.* to hang up
auflösen to dissolve
aufmachen to open
aufnehmen *st.v.* to take in, to pick
  up
aufpassen to watch, pay attention,
  look after
aufpumpen to pump up

aufreissen *st.v.* to tear open, rip
aufschlagen *st.v.* to add, to raise
  (the price), to open (a book)
aufschliessen *st.v.* to unlock
aufschreiben *st.v.* to write down
aufsetzen to put on, to set upon
aufsparen to save for
aufstehen *st.v.* to get up, rise
aufsuchen to look up
aufwachen to wake up
aufziehen *st.v.* to wind (watch)
Auge,-n *n.* eye
Augenblick,-e *m.* moment
Augenbraue,-n *f.* eyebrow
August *m.* August
aus out of, from
Ausbildung,-en training,
  development
Ausdruck,-¨e *m.* expression
ausdrücken to express
auseinanderfallen *st.v.* to fall apart
Ausfuhr,-en *f.* export
ausfüllen to fill out
ausgebrannt burned out
Ausgang,-¨e *m.* exit
ausgezeichnet excellent
ausgleichen *st.v.* to adjust, equalize
Auskunftsstelle,-n *f.* information
  desk
Ausländer,- *m.* foreigner
Ausländerin,-nen *f.* foreigner
auspacken to unpack
ausprobieren to try out
ausruhen *refl.* to rest, to take a rest
ausschalten to switch off, to turn off
aussehen *st.v.* to look, to appear
aussen outside
Aussenkabine,-n *f.* outside cabin
ausser beside(s), except
ausserdem besides
ausserhalb outside of
ausserordentlich extraordinary
ausspielen to lead (card game)
aussteigen *st.v.* to descend, get off
aussuchen to pick out, select
austauschen to exchange
ausüben to exert
Ausverkauf,-¨e *m.* sale
ausverkauft sold out
Auswanderer,- *m.* emigrant
Ausweispapiere *pl.* identification
  papers

auszupfen to pluck
Auto,-s n. automobile
Autobahn,-en f. highway (auto)
Autobahnkarte,-n f. road map
Automobil,-e n. automobile
Autotour,-en f. auto trip

B

Backe,-n f. cheek
Backfisch,-e m. girl in her teens, adolescent girl
Backpflaume,-n f. prunes
Backzahn,-"e m. back tooth
Badetuch,-"er n. bath towel
Badezimmer,- n. bathroom
Bahnhof,-"e m. station (railroad)
Bahnsteig,-e m. platform
bald soon, presently
Balkon,-s m. balcony
Bank,-en f. bank
Bann,- m. spell
Barbier,-e m. barber
Barbiergeschäft,-e n. barber shop
Barbierladen,- m. barber shop
Base,-n f. cousin, feminine
Bau,-s,-ten m. building, structure, style
Bauart,-en f. architecture
bauen to build
Bauer,-s,-n m. farmer, peasant
Baukunst f. architecture
Baum,-"e m. tree
Bauwerk,-e n. building
Bayern Bavaria
bayrisch Bavarian
bedecken to cover
bedeuten to mean
bedeutend significant
Bedeutung,-en f. importance
Bedienung,-en f. service
beilegen to add, enclose
beeilen refl. to hurry
beeindrucken to impress
befestigt fortified
Befestigung,-en f. fortification
befinden refl. st.v. to be
befriedigen to satisfy
beginnen st.v. to begin
begleiten to accompany
begnügen mit refl. to be content with

begrenzt limited
bei at the house of, by, at
beide both
Bein,-e n. leg
beinah(e) almost
beitragen st.v. to contribute
beiwohnen to attend
bekannt known, familiar
Bekannte,-n m. & f. acquaintance
bekanntmachen to introduce
Bekanntschaft,-en f. acquaintance
bekommen st.v. to get, receive
bemerken to notice
benachrichtigen to notify, inform
Benzin n. gasoline
Benzintank,-e m. gas tank
Benzinverbrauch m. gasoline consumption
beobachten to watch, observe
bequem comfortable
Bequemlichkeit,-en f. comfort
beraten st.v. to give advice
bereit ready, prepared
bereiten to cause; to prepare
bereits already
Berg- und Talbahn,-en f. roller coaster
Bergriese,-n m. very high mountain
Bergsee,-n m. mountain lake
berichten to report
beruhigt comforted
berühmt famous
beschäftigen to occupy
beschwingt winged
besetzt busy, crowded
besingen st.v. to sing of
Besitz,-e m. possession
besohlen to put soles on
besonders especially
besorgen to attend to, get
besser better
Besserung, gute speedy recovery
Bestecke pl. knives, forks, and spoons
bestehen st.v. to exist
bestellen to order, give a message
bestimmt definite
Besuch,-e m. visit
besuchen to visit
beten to pray
Betrag,-"e m. amount, sum
Bett,-s,-en n. bed

bevor *conj.* before
bewaffnet provided; armed
Bewegung,-en *f.* motion
bewölkt sein to be cloudy
bewundern to admire
bezahlen to pay
bezaubern to enchant
beziehen auf *refl.st.v.* to refer to
Biegung,-en *f.* turn
Bier,-e *n.* beer
Bild,-er *n.* picture
bilden to form
billig cheap
Birne,-n *f.* pear; electric bulb
bis till, until, to
bisher up to now
bisschen, ein some, a little
bitte please; you are welcome
bitten *st.v.* to beg, ask for
bitten um to ask for
bitter bitter
blau blue
bleiben *st.v.* to remain, stay
bleichen *st.v.* to bleach
Bleistift,-e *m.* pencil
Blitz,-e *m.* lightning
blitzen to lighten, flash
Blume,-n *f.* flower
Blumenkohl,-e *m.* cauliflower
Bluse,-n *f.* blouse
Blutdruck *m.* blood pressure
Blüte,-n *f.* height; flower; blossom
Bohne,-n *f.* bean
   grüne Bohnen *pl.* green beans
Böse *n.* evil, bad
böse sein to be angry
Branche,-n *f.* branch, specialty
Bratkartoffeln *pl.* fried potatoes
brauchen to need
braun brown
Brei *m.* cereal (hot)
breit broad
Bremse,-n *f.* brake
Brett,-er *n.* board
Brief,-e *m.* letter
Briefmarken,-n *f.* stamp
Briefumschlag,-"e *m.* envelope
bringen *irr.w.v.* to bring
Brote,-e *n.* bread, loaves of bread
Brötchen,- *n.* roll
Brücke,-en *f.* bridge
Bruder,-" *m.* brother

Brüderlichkeit *f.* fraternity
Brüderschaft,-en *f.* good fellowship
Brunnen,- *m.* fountain
buntbemalt painted in many colors
Burg,-en *f.* stronghold
Büro,-s *n.* office
Büroraum,-"e office room
Bürste,-n *f.* brush
bürsten to brush
Bus,-se *m.* bus
Büstenhalter,- *m.* brassiere
Butter *f.* butter
Butterbrot,-e *n.* bread and butter

D

da *conj.* since (reason), inasmuch
da *adv.* there; then
Dach,-"er *n.* roof
damals at that time
Dame,-n *f.* lady
Damenkonfektion *f.* store specializing in ladies clothes
Damenmantel,-" *m.* lady's coat
damit so that; with that, with it
Dampfer,- *m.* steamer
danach after that
dankbar grateful
danke thanks, thank you
danken to thank
dann then
darbieten *st.v.* to offer
darüber over it, above it
darum therefore
das the *n.*; that, which
dass *conj.* that
dasselbe the same
Datum, Daten *n.* date
dauern to last
Dauerwelle,-n *f.* permanent wave
davon from it, of it
dazu to that, to it
Deck,-e *m.* deck
denken *irr.w.v.* to think
Denkmal,-"er *n.* monument
denn *conj.* because, for
der the *m.*; who
derb heavy, coarse
Deutsche *m. & f.* (the) German
Deutschland *n.* Germany
Dezember *m.* December
Dichter,- *m.* poet

die the f.; who
dienen to serve
Dienst,-e m. service
Dienstag,-e m. Tuesday
dies this
dieser this, this one
diktieren to dictate
doch still, yet
Donner,- m. thunder
Donnerstag,-e m. Thursday
Dorf,-"er n. village
dort there
drall robust
Drittel, ein a third
Drogist,-en m. druggist
Droschke,-n f. taxi, cab
drüben over there, yonder
drücken to pinch, press
dunkel dark
dunkelblau dark blue
durch through, by
Durchgang,-"e m. way through, passage
D-Zug,-"e (Durchgangszug) express train
dürfen mod. to be permitted, may
duzen to call a person thou

E

ebenfalls also
ebenso just so, just, the same
echt real, genuine
Ecke,-n f. corner
ehe before
eher rather
Ei,-er n. egg
eigen own
eigenartig odd, peculiar
ein a, one
einbiegen st.v. to turn into
eindringen st.v. to penetrate
Eindruck,-"e m. impression
eindrucksvoll impressive
einfach simple, plain
Einfachheit f. simplicity
einfallen st.v. to occur, to interrupt
Einfamilienhaus,-"er n. one-family house
einflössen st.v. to instill, inspire
Einfluss,-"e m. influence
Einfuhr,-en f. import

einführen to import, introduce
Eingang,-"e m. entrance
einhaken to interlock
Einheit,-en f. unit, unity
einige few, a few
Einkauf,-"e m. purchase
  Einkäufe machen to go shopping
einladen st.v. to invite
Einladung,-en f. invitation
einlösen to redeem
einmal once
einmalig happening once
einpacken to pack
Einreiseerlaubnis,- f. permit of entry
einschalten to switch on, to turn on
einschlafen st.v. to fall asleep
Einschreibebrief,-e m. registered letter
einschreiben st.v. to register
einsteigen st.v. to get into; to enter
einstellen auf to be geared to
eintreten st.v. to enter
Eintritt,-e m. entrance
Eintrittskarte,-n f. admission ticket
einverstanden sein to agree
Einwanderer,- m. immigrant
einwechseln to give in exchange
Einwohner,- m. inhabitant
Einzelzimmer,- n. single room
einziehen st.v. to lace, pull in
einzig only
einzigartig unique
Eisenbahn,-en f. railroad
Eiswasser n. ice water
Eltern pl. parents
empfehlen st.v. to recommend
Empfehlung,-en f. recommendation
Empfehlungsbrief,-e m. letter of recommendation
empfinden st.v. to feel
Ende,-s,-n n. end
enden to end
endlich at last, finally
eng narrow, light
Engel,- m. angel
England n. England
Engländer,- m. Englishman
Enkel,- m. grandson
entfernt remote
entlang along

entschuldigen to excuse
entsetzt horrified
entweder . . . oder either . . . or
entzünden to inflame
Entzündung,-en f...inflammation
entwickeln develop
er he
Erbse,-n f. pea
    grüne Erbsen pl. green peas
Erdbeere,-n f. strawberry
Erdgeschoss,-e n. ground floor
erfahren st.v. to experience
erfrischend refreshing
erfüllen to fulfill
erhalten st.v. to preserve; to receive
erhöhen to increase
Erholung f. recreation
erinnern refl. to remind of
erkennen irr.w.v. to perceive, see,
    know, understand, recognize
Erkenntnis,-se f. understanding;
    perception
erklären to explain
Erklärung,-en f. explanation
erleben to experience
Erlebnis,-se n. adventure,
    experience
erledigen to take care of
erlösen to save
Erlösung f. deliverance
ermuntern to encourage
ernst serious, earnest
erobern to conquer
erreichen to reach
erscheinen st.v. to appear
erschöpft exhausted
erschrecken st.v. to be frightened
erst not till; at first
erstens firstly
erwachsen grown-up
erwarten to expect
erzählen to tell, relate
es it
Essen,- n. food, meal, eating
essen st.v. to eat
Essig m. vinegar
Esszimmer,- n. dining room
etwas a little, some
Europa n. Europe
Examen,- n. examination
existieren to exist
exportieren to export

F

fahren st.v. to ride, to travel
Fahrer,- m. driver
Fahrkarte,-n f. ticket
Fahrplan,-"e m. timetable
Fahrrad,-"er n. bicycle
Fahrstuhl,-"e m. elevator
Fahrt,-en f. trip
Fall,-"e m. case
falls in case
falsch false
    . . . gehen to be wrong (watch)
Farbe,-n f. color
färben to dye
fast almost
Februar m. February
Feder,-n f. feather, spring
fehlen to be missing, lacking
Fenster,- n. window
Fensterladen,-" m. shutter
Ferne f. distance
Fernsprecher,- m. telephone
fertig ready, finished
festschnallen refl. to buckle on,
    fasten
Festspiel,-e n. festival
Festung,-en f. fortress
Festungswall,-"e m. rampart
Feuer n. fire
Feuerzeug,-e n. lighter
Fieber n. fever
Figur,-en f. figure (shape)
Film,-e m. film
Filzhut,-"e m. felt hat
finden st.v. to find
Finger,- m. finger
Firma, Firmen f. firm
Fisch,-e m. fish
Fischerdorf,-"er n. fishing village
Fischgericht,-e n. fish course
Flasche,-n f. bottle
Fleisch n. meat, flesh
Fleischbrühe,-n f. meat broth
fliehen st.v. to flee
Fluch,-"e m. curse
Flügel m. grand piano
Flughafen m. airport
Flugkarte,-n f. flight ticket
Flugplatz,-"e m. airfield
Flugzeug,-e n. airplane
Flunder,-n f. flounder

Fluss,-"e *m.* river
flüstern to whisper
folgen to follow
Form,-en *f.* form, shape
förmlich formal
Formular,-e *n.* form, blank
Fracht,-en *f.* freight
Frachtdampfer *m.* freighter
Frachtschiff,-e *n.* freighter
fragen to ask
Frankreich *n.* France
Franzose,-n *m.* Frenchman
Frau,-en *f.* woman, wife, Mrs.
frei free
Freitag,-e *m.* Friday
Fremdenverkehr *m.* tourist trade
Fremdenzimmer *n.* guest room
Fremdsprache,-n *f.* foreign language
Freude,-n *f.* joy
freuen *refl.* to be glad, to rejoice
Freund,-e *m.* friend
Freundin,-nen *f.* friend
freundlich kind, friendly
Freundschaft,-en *f.* friendship
Frikassee von Huhn *n.* chicken
  fricassee
frisch fresh
Friseur,-e *m.* hairdresser
Friseuse,-n *f.* hairdresser
frisieren to dress a person's hair
Frisiersalon,-s *m.* hairdressing salon
Frisiertisch,-e *m.* dressing table
Frisur,-en *f.* dressing of the hair;
  hair-do
froh happy, glad
fröhlich cheerful, merry, happy
Fröhlichkeit *f.* cheerfulness
früh early
früher formerly, earlier
Frühling,-e *m.* spring
Frühstück,-e *n.* breakfast
fühlen to feel
  sich ... to feel (well, etc.)
führen to lead, carry (store)
Führung,-en *f.* guidance
füllen to fill
Füllfeder,-n *f.* fountain pen
fungieren to act
für for
fürchten to fear
  sich ... vor to be afraid of
Fuss,-"e *m.* foot

G

Gabel,-n *f.* fork
Gang,-"e *m.* course, dish; passage-
  way; gear (car)
ganz complete(ly), all
Garderobe,-n *f.* wardrobe
Gardine,-n *f.* curtain
Garten,-" *m.* garden
Gässchen,- *n.* alley
Gast,-"e *m.* guest
Gasthaus,-"er *n.* restaurant
Gatte,-n *m.* husband
Gaumen,- *m.* gum
Gebäude,-n *n.* building
geben *st.v.* to give, deal (cards)
  es gibt there are
geboren born
Gebrauch,-"e *m.* use, custom
gebrochen broken
Gebühr,-en *f.* fee
Geburt,-en *f.* birth
Geburtsstätte,-n place of birth
Gefahr,-en *f.* danger
gefallen *st.v.* to like,
  to be pleased
Gefrorenes *n.* ice cream
gegen against, toward
Gegensatz,-"e *m.* antagonism;
  contrast
gegenseitig mutual
gegenüber opposite
Gegenwart *f.* presence, present
  (tense)
Geheimnis,-se *n.* secret
gehen *st.v.* to go, walk
gehören to belong
gehören *refl.* to be proper
Geist,-er *m.* spirit; intellect
geisteskrank insane
geistig intellectual
Gelächter,- *n.* laughter
Geld *n.* money
Gelee,-s *n.* jelly
Gelegenheit,-en *f.* opportunity
geloben to vow
Gelübde,- *n.* vow
Gemahlin,-nen *f.* wife
Gemälde,- *n.* painting
Gemäldesammlung,-en *f.* collection
  of paintings
gemeinsam joint, in common

gemütlich cozy, comfortable, congenial
Gemütlichkeit f. joviality
geniessen st.v. to enjoy
genug enough
Gepäck n. baggage
   das ... aufgeben to check the luggage
Gepäckannahme,-n f. luggage office
Gepäcknetz,-e n. luggage rack
Gepäckträger,- m. porter
Gepäckzettel,- m. baggage label
Gepräge,- n. feature
gerade just now, exactly
geradeaus straight ahead
geradeüber just across, opposite
Geräusch,-e n. noise
gering little, small, slight
gern gladly, like
Geschäft,-e n. business
Geschäftsfreund,-e m. business connection
Geschäftshaus,-̈er n. commercial firm, office building
Geschäftsreise,-n f. business trip
Geschäftszweig,-e m. specialty, branch
geschehen st.v. to happen
Geschichte,-n f. story, history
geschichtlich historical
Geschlecht,-er n. sex, gender
Geschmack,-̈e m. taste
Geschmacksache f. matter of taste
Gesellschaft,-en f. company, party
Gesicht,-er n. face
Gestalt,-en f. figure
gestehen st.v. to confess
gestern yesterday
Getränk,-e n. beverage
gewaltig powerful, mighty
gewiss certain
gewissermassen so to say
Gewitter,- n. thunderstorm
Giebel,- m. gable
Gier f. greed
Gipfel,- m. peak, top, summit
Glas,-̈er n. glass
Glaswaren pl. glassware
glauben to believe, think
gleich directly, immediately
Gleichberechtigung f. equality
gleichzeitig at the same time

Glied,-er n. limb
Glück n. happiness
glücklich happy, fortunate
glücklicherweise fortunately
gnädige Frau madame
golden of gold
göttlich divine
Graben,- m. ditch
graben st.v. to dig
gratis free of charge
gratulieren to congratulate
grau gray
Grenze,-n f. frontier, borders
gross great, large
grossartig grand
Grösse,-n f. size
Grösse,-n f. size, height; greatness
Grosstadt,-̈e f. metropolis
Grossvater,-̈ m. grandfather
grün green
Gründer,- m. founder
gründlich thorough, thoroughly
Gruppe,-n f. group
grüssen to greet, send regards
Grütze,- f. cereal (hot)
Gummischuh,-e m. rubber, rubbers
gut good, well

H

Haar,-e n. hair
Haaröl,-e n. hair oil
Haarwasser,- n. hair tonic
haben irr.v. to have
Hacken,- m. heel
Hafen,-̈ m. harbor
Hafenstadt,-̈e f. seaport
Haferbrei m. oatmeal
halb half
Halbes, ein a half
Hälfte, die the half
Hals,-̈e m. throat, neck
halten st.v. to hold, keep, stop
haltmachen to stop
Hammelkeule,-n f. leg of lamb
Hammelkotelett,-s n. lamb chop
Handelsstadt,-̈e f. commercial city
Handgeld,-er n. deposit
Handgepäck,-e n. hand luggage
Handkoffer,- m. suitcase
Händler,- m. dealer
Handschuh,-e m. glove

Handtuch,-"er n. towel (hand)
hart hard
hässlich ugly
Hauptbahnhof,-"e main terminal
Hauptstadt,-"e f. capital
Hauptstrasse,-n f. main street
Hauptverkehrsstrasse,-n f. main road
Haus,-"er n. house
Hausfrau,-en f. housewife
heben st.v. to lift, raise
heilig holy
Heimat,-en f. native country
Heimweh n. homesickness
heissen st.v. to be called, named
helfen st.v. to help
hell light, bright
hellblau light blue
herantreten an st.v. to step up to
herausfallen st.v. to fall out
herausgeben st.v. to give change, to give up
herauskommen st.v. to come out; to be one's turn
herausnehmen st.v. to take out
Herbst,-e m. fall
herein Come in!
hereinbekommen st.v. to get in
Herr,-en m. master, gentleman, Mister
Herrenwäsche pl. men's underwear and shirts
Herrenzimmer,- n. den (room)
herrlich splendid
herrschen to reign, prevail
herumfahren st.v. to ride around
herumlaufen st.v. to run around
Herz,-ens,-en n. heart
herzlich cordially, heartily
heute today
heutig today's, present
hier here
hierher here (direction to place)
Hilfe f. help
Himbeereis n. raspberry ice
Himmel,- m. sky, heaven
hinauf upward
hinaufsteigen st.v. to step up, ascend
hinaus out, outside (go), out into
hinein into
hineinreichen to reach into

hingeben refl. st.v. to indulge
hinten in the rear, behind
hinter behind
Hinterkopf,-"e back of the head
Hinterzimmer,- n. backroom
hinunter downward
hinuntergehen st.v. to go down
hoch high
hochachtungsvoll respectfully, truly yours
Hochbahn,-en f. elevated railroad
Hochzeitsreise,-n f. wedding trip
hoffentlich I hope, it is to be hoped
holprig uneven
Honorar,-e n. fee
hören to hear, listen
Hose,-n f. trousers, pants
Hotel,-s hotel
Hotelhalle,-n f. hotel lobby
hübsch pretty, nice
gebratene Huhn,-"er n. roast chicken
Hühnersuppe,-n f. chicken soup
Hund,-e m. dog
Hundermarkschein,-e m. hundred mark bill
Hunger m. hunger
hungrig hungry
Hut,-"e m. hat
Hutabteilung,-en f. hat department
hüten refl. w.v. to be careful

I

ich I
Idee,-n f. idea
Ideenaustausch,-"e m. exchange of ideas
immer always
importieren to import
in in, into
indem while
Inhaber,- m. owner
innerhalb within
interessant interesting
inzwischen in the meantime
irgendeinmal at one time or another
Italien n. Italy
Italiener,- m. Italian

J

ja yes
Jacke,-n f. jacket
jagen to hunt
Jahr,-e n. year
jahrelang for years
Jahrhundert,-e n. century
Jammer,- m. calamity
Januar m. January
je ... desto the ... the
jedenfalls in any case, by all means
jeder each one, each
jederzeit any time
jener that one
jetzt now
Jubel m. jubilation
Jugend f. youth (period of life)
Juli m. July
jung young
Junge,-n m. boy
Juni m. June

K

Kabarett,-s n. cabaret
Kabine,-n f. cabin, stateroom
Kabinenkoffer,- m. stateroom trunk
Kabinennummer,- f. cabin number
Kaffee m. coffee
Käfig,-e m. cage
Kajüte,-n f. cabin, stateroom
kahl bleak, bare
Kaiser,- m. emperor
Kaiserreich,-e n. empire
Kalbsbraten,- m. roast of veal
Kalbsleber f. calf's liver
Kamel,-e n. camel
Kamm,-¨e m. comb
kämmen to comb
Kampf,-¨e m. struggle
kämpfen to fight
Kapelle,-n f. band
  (of musicians)
Karotte,-n f. carrot
Karpfen,- m. carp
Karte,-n f. card, ticket
  Karten mischen to shuffle cards
  Karten spielen to play cards
Kartoffel,-n f. potato
Kartoffelbrei m. mashed potatoes
Kartoffelklösse, pl. potato
  dumplings

Karton,-s m. carton
Käse,- m. cheese
Katze,-n f. cat
kaufen to buy
kaum hardly
Kekse f. cookies
Kellner,- m. waiter
Kellnerin,-nen f. waitress
kennen irr.w.v. to know (a person,
  place)
kennenlernen to get acquainted,
  meet
Kerl,-e m. fellow
Kind,-er n. child
Kindheit,-en f. childhood
Kino,-s n. movies
Kirche,-n f. church
klagen complain
klappen to go well
klar clear
Klasse,-n f. class
Klavier,-e n. piano
kleben to stick, paste
Kleid,-er n. dress
Kleiderschrank,-¨e m. wardrobe
Kleidung,-en f. clothes
klein small, little
Kleingeld n. small change
Kleinigkeit,-en f. little matter
Kleinkunstbühne,-n f. cabaret
klingen st.v. to ring
klopfen to knock
Knabe,-n m. boy
Knopf,-¨e m. button
Koffer,- m. trunk
Kofferraum,-¨e m. baggage
  compartment
kommen st.v. to come
Kommode,-n f. dresser
komponieren to compose
Komponist,-en m. composer
Kompott,-e n. stewed fruit
können to be able, can
Kontor,-e n. office
Kopf,-¨e m. head
Kopfschmerz,-es,-en m. headache
kopfschüttelnd shaking one's head
Kopf,-¨e waschen m. to shampoo
Korb,-¨e m. basket
Korrespondenz,-en f.
  correspondence
Korridor,-e m. hall, floor

Korsett,-s *n.* girdle, corset
kosten to cost
Kraft,-̈e *f.* strength, power
Kraftwagen,- *m.* automobile
Kragen,- *m.* collar
krank sick
Krankenhaus,-̈er *n.* hospital
Krankenwagen,- *m.* ambulance
Krempe,-n *f.* brim
kreuzen to cross
Krieg,-e *m.* war
Krug,-̈e *m.* pitcher
krumm winding; crooked
Küche,-n *f.* kitchen
Kuchen,- *m.* cake
Kuh,-̈e *f.* cow
Kühler,- *m.* radiator
Kultur,-en *f.* culture
Kunst,-̈e *f.* art
Künstler,- *m.* artist
künstlerisch artistic
Kunstwerk,-e *n.* work of art
Kupferstecher,- *m.* engraver
Kupplung,-en *f.* clutch
Kurs,-e *m.* rate of exchange
kurz short
Kusin,-s *m.* cousin
Kusine,-n *f.* cousin
Kuss,-̈e *m.* kiss
küssen to kiss
Kuvert,-s *m.* envelope

L

lächeln to smile
lachen to laugh
Laden,-̈ *m.* store
Lage,-n *f.* site, situation
Lampe,-n *f.* lamp
Land,-̈er *n.* country, land
landen to land
Landschaft,-en *f.* landscape
Landkarte,-n *f.* map
lang long
Länge,-n *f.* length
lassen *st.v.* to let
laufen *st.v.* to run
leben to live
Leben,- *n.* life
Leber,- *f.* liver
lebhaft lively
Lederwaren *f. pl.* leather goods

ledig unmarried
legen to lay, put
Lehrer,- *m.* teacher
lehrreich instructive
leicht easy, light
leichtlebig happy-go-lucky
Leiden,- *n.* suffering
leider unfortunately, alas
Leitung,-en *f.* connection, line,
   management
lernen to learn
lesen *st.v.* to read
letzt last
leuchtend shining
Leute *pl.* people
Licht,-e *n.* light
   elektrisches ... electric light
Lichtmaschine,-n *f.* generator
Liebe *f.* love
liebenswürdig charming, kind
lieber rather, to prefer
lieblich lovely
Lieblingslied,-er *n.* favorite song
Lied,-er *n.* song, carol
liegen *st.v.* to lie
Liegestuhl,-̈e *m.* deck chair
Likör,-e *m.* cordial
links left
loben to praise
Loch,-̈er *n.* hole
Löffel,- *m.* spoon
Loge,-n *f.* box (in theater)
Löschblatt,-̈er *n.* blotter
losfahren *st.v.* to start (on vehicle)
losgehen *st.v.* to get started,
   come off
loswerden *st.v.* to get rid off
Löwe,-n *m.* lion
Luft *f.* air
Luftpostbrief,-e *m.* air mail letter
Luftpostkarte,-n *f.* air mail postal
   card
Luftpostleichtbrief,-e *m.*
   air mail letter
Lunge,-n *f.* lung
Lust *f.* desire
lustig gay, jolly
Lyriker,- *m.* lyric poet

M

machen to make, do

Macht,-ˉe f. power
mächtig mighty, powerful
Mädchen,- n. girl, servant girl
Magen,- m. stomach
Mahlzeit,-en f. meal
Mai m. May
Maler,- m. painter
Malerei,-en f. painting
malnehmen st.v. to multiply
mancher many a
Manchette,-n f. cuff
Mandel,-n f. tonsil; almond
Maniküre,-n f. manicure
maniküren to manicure
Mann,-ˉer m. man
männlich masculine
Mantel,-ˉ m. coat, topcoat
Mappe,-n f. brief case
Märchenwelt f. world of romance
Mark f. mark
Marmelade,-n f. marmalade, jam
März m. March
Mauer,-n f. wall (outside)
Maus,-ˉe f. mouse
Mechaniker,- m. mechanic
Medizin,-en f. medicine
mehr more
mehr als more than
Meile,-n f. mile
meinen to mean
meistens mostly
Meisterwerk,-e n. masterpiece
Mensch,-en m. human being
merken to notice
sich ... to remember
messen to measure
Messer,- n. knife
mieten to rent
Mietshaus,-ˉer n. apartment house
Milch f. milk
Minute,-n f. minute
Missverständnis,-se n. misunder-
  standing
mit with
mitbringen irr.w.v. to bring
  (with one)
Mitleid,- n. compassion
miteinander with each other
Mittag,-e m. noon, midday
Mittagessen n. dinner, lunch
mittags at noon

Mitte,-n f. middle
Mittel,- n. means
Mittelalter n. Middle Ages
Mitteldeutschland n. Central
  Germany
Mittelpunkt,-e m. center
Mitternacht,-ˉe f. midnight
Mittlerin,-nen f. middleman
Mittwoch m. Wednesday
mitwirken to contribute to
Möbel pl. furniture
möblieren to furnish
mögen to like, may
möglich possible
Möglichkeit,-en f. possibility
möglichst if possible
Monat,-e m. month
Montag,-e m. Monday
Morgen,- m. morning
morgen tomorrow
morgens in the morning
Mostrich m. mustard
Motorboot,-e motor boat
Motorrad,-ˉer n. motorcycle
müde tired
multiplizieren to multiply
Mund,-ˉer m. mouth
Mundwasser,- n. mouth wash
munter lively, brisk
Musik f. music
Muskel,-n f. muscle
müssen must
Mutter,-ˉ f. mother

N

nach after, to (place), according to
nachdem conj. after
nachgehen st.v. to be slow (watch);
  to follow
nachher afterwards
nachholen to catch up on
Nachmittag,-e m. afternoon
  Spätnachmittag,-e m. late
    afternoon
nachmittags in the afternoon
Nachmittagszug,-ˉe m. afternoon
  train
nachsehen st.v. to check;
  to look after
nächst next
Nacht,-ˉe f. night

Nachtisch,-e *m.* dessert
nachts at night
Nachttisch,-e *m.* night table
Nacken,- *m.* neck
Nagel,- *m.* nail
nageln to nail
Nagelpolitur,-en *f.* nail polish
Nagelschere,-n *f.* nail scissors
Nähe *f.* nearness
  in der . . . near, in the
  neighborhood
nahekommen *st.v.* to come close to
nähen to sew, stitch
näherkommen *st.v.* to come closer
nähern *refl. v.* to approach
Naht,-"e *f.* (s) seam
Name,-n *m.* name
Nase,-n *f.* nose
Natur *f.* nature
natürlich naturally
neben next to, near
nebenan next door
Nebenfluss,-"e *m.* tributary
necken to tease
Neffe,-n *m.* nephew
nehmen *st.v.* to take
neigen to be inclined
nein no
nennen *irr.w.v.* to call, name
Nerv,-en *m.* nerve
nett nice, pretty, lovely
neu new
Neubau,-s,-ten *m.* rebuilding
Neuste *n.* the latest thing
Neuzeit *f.* modern times
nicht not
nicht mehr anymore
Nichte,-n *f.* niece
nicken to nod
niedlich cute
niemand nobody
Niederlage,-n *f.* defeat
noch yet, still
noch ein(e) another one
nochmals once again
Norden *m.* north
Norwegen *n.* Norway
Norweger,- *m.* Norwegian
Not *f.* need, distress
nötig necessary
Nötige *n.* the necessary thing

November *m.* November
Nummer,- *f.* number
numerieren to number
nun now
nur only

O

ob whether, if
oben above, upstairs
  nach . . . (to go) upstairs
  von . . . from the top
Oberhemd,-s,-en *n.* shirt
obgleich although
Obst *n.* fruit
oder or
öffentlich public
oft often
ohne without
Ohr,-s,-en *n.* ear
Oktober *m.* October
Öl *n.* oil
ölen to oil, grease
Omnibus,-se *m.* bus
Onkel,- *m.* uncle
Oper,-n *f.* opera
Opfer,- *n.* sacrifice, victim
Orange,-n *f.* orange
Orangensaft,-"e *m.* orange juice
Ordnung,-en *f.* order
Originalwerk,-e *n.* original work
Ort,-e *m.* spot
Osten *m.* east
Österreich *n.* Austria
Österreicher,- *m.* Austrian
Ozeandampfer,- *m.* ocean liner

P

Paar,-e *n.* pair, couple
  ein paar a few
paarmal, ein several times
Panne,-n *f.* flat tire
Papier,-e *n.* paper
Park,-e *m.* park
Pass,-"e *m.* passport
passen to fit, suit
passieren to pass, go on, happen
Passionsspiel,-e *n.* Passion Play
Passkontrolle,-n *f.* passport control
patent smart

Personenzug,-ˮe *m.* local train
persönlich personal
Pest *f.* pestilence
Pflasterstein,-e *m.* cobble stone
Pfeffer *m.* pepper
Pfeife,-n *f.* whistle, pipe
Pfennig,-e *m.* penny
Pferd,-e *n.* horse
Pfirsich,-e *m.* peach
Pflaume,-n *f.* plum
Pflaumenkompott,-e *n.* stewed
    plums (prunes)
Piano,-s *n.* piano
planen to plan
Platz,-ˮe *m.* seat, square
Platzkarte,-n *f.* ticket for a reserved
    seat
plaudern to chat
Plombe,-n *f.* filling (tooth)
plombieren to fill (tooth)
plötzlich suddenly
Pole,-n *m.* Pole
Polen *n.* Poland
Polizei *f.* Police
Pompelmus,-e *f.* grapefruit
Portwein,-e *m.* port wine
Porzellan,-e *n.* china, porcelain
Postamt,-ˮer *n.* post-office
Postkarte,-n *f.* postal card
Preis,-e *m.* price
preiswert worth the money, cheap
Privatkontor,-e *n.* private office
Prosit (Prost) your health
Prozent,-e *n.* percent
Publikum *n.* people, public
    spectators
Punkt,-e *m.* point, dot
putzen to shine; to clean

Q

Qualität,-en *f.* quality

R

Rad,-ˮer *n.* bicycle, wheel
Rasierklinge,-n *f.* razor blade
Rasierpinsel,- *m.* shaving brush
Rasierseife,-n *f.* shaving soap
raten *st.v.* to advise, guess
Rathaus,-ˮer *n.* city hall

Ratte,-n *f.* rat
rauchen to smoke
Raucherabteil,-e *n.* smoking
    compartment
Rauchsalon,-s smoking room
Raum,-ˮe *m.* room, space
rechnen to figure, calculate
Rechnung,-en *f.* bill
Rechnungsbetrag,-ˮe amount of bill
recht very, right
rechts right (direction)
Regen *m.* rain
Regenmantel,-ˮ raincoat
Regenschirm,-e *m.* umbrella
regnen to rain
reich rich
reichen to reach
Reichsversammlung *f.* congress of
    the empire
Reichtum,-ˮer *m.* wealth
Reifen,- *m.* tire
reihen an *refl. v.* to put in a row
rein clean, pure
reinigen to clean
Reis *m.* rice
Reise,-n *f.* trip, voyage
Reiseamt,-ˮer *n.* official travel
    bureau
Reisebüro,-s *n.* travel bureau
Reiseerlebnis,-se *n.* traveling
    experience
Reisegefährte,-n *m.* traveling
    companion
reisen to travel
Reisecheck,-s *m.* travelers' check
Reisetasche,-n *f.* traveling bag
Reiz,-e *m.* charm
reizend charming
Reparatur,-en *f.* repairs
reparieren to repair
reservieren to reserve
Rest,-e *m.* rest, remainder
Rettung,-en *f.* salvation
Rezept,-e *n.* prescription
Rheinwein,-e *m.* Rhine wine
richtig gehen *st.v.* to be right
    (watch)
Riese,-n *m.* giant
Riesenrad,-ˮer *n.* ferris wheel
riesig enormous
Ring,-e *m.* ring

riskieren to risk
Ritter,- m. knight
Rock,-¨e m. skirt
Roggenbrot,-e n. rye bread
Röntgenaufnahme,-n f. X-ray
  photograph
rosa pink
rot red
Rotkohl m. red cabbage
Rotwein,-e m. red wine
Rücken,- m. back
Rückenlicht,-e n. tail light
Rückkehr f. return
Rucksack,-¨e m. knapsack
Rückweg,-e m. way back
Ruderboot,-e n. rowboat
Ruf m. reputation
rufen st.v. to call, shout
ruhen to rest
ruhig calm, quiet
Rührei,-er n. scrambled egg
rührend touching
rund round
Russe,-n m. Russian
Russland n. Russia

S

Saal (pl. Säle) m. hall, large room
Sache,-n f. thing, matter
  getragene . . . pl. worn clothes
  (used)
Saft,-¨e m. juice
sagen to say
Sahne f. cream
Salat,-e m. salad, lettuce
Salz,-e n. salt
Salzkartoffeln pl. boiled potatoes
sammeln to gather
Samstag,-e m. Saturday
Saum,-¨e m. hem, seam
sausen to whiz along
schaffen st.v. to make, create
schallend roaring
Schalter,- m. switch; ticket window
Schatten,- m. shade
schattig shady
Schauspieler,- m. actor
Schauspielerin,-nen f. actress
Schauspielkunst f. art of acting
Scheck,-s m. check
Scheibe,-n f. slice

Schein,-e m. bill
scheinbar seemingly
scheinen st.v. to seem, appear
Scheitel,- m. part (of hair), crown
  of head
schelten st.v. to scold
scherzen to joke
Scheu f. awe
Schicksal,-e n. fate
schiefgetreten worn down
  (on one side)
Schiff,-e n. ship
Schiffsfahrkarte,-n f. steamer ticket
Schild,-er n. sign
Schimmer,- m. glamour
Schinken m. ham
Schlaf m. sleep
Schläfe,-n f. temple
schlafen st.v. to sleep
Schlafzimmer,- n. bedroom
schlagen st.v. to strike, beat
Schlange,-n f. snake
schlapp low; limp
schlecht bad, badly
schliesslich finally
schlimm bad
Schlips,-e m. necktie
Schloss,-¨er n. castle
Schlüssel,- m. key
schmecken to taste
Schmerz,-es,-en m. pain
schmutzig dirty, soiled
Schnee,- snow
schneebedeckt snow covered
schneiden st.v. to cut
schnell fast, quick
Schnelldampfer,- m. fast steamer
Schnellzug,-¨e m. express train
Schnitte,-n f. slice
  eine . . . (Scheibe) Brot a slice of
  bread
Schnürsenkel,- m. shoelace
Schokolade f. chocolate
schon already
schön beautiful
Schönheit,-en f. beauty
Schornstein,-e m. chimney
Schrank,-¨e m. closet
schreiben st.v. to write
Schreibmaschine,-n f. typewriter
Schreibpult,-e n. writing desk

Schritt,-e m. step, pace
Schublade,-n f. drawer
Schuh,-e m. shoe
Schuhmacher,- m. shoemaker
Schule,-n f. school
Schüler,- m. pupil
Schutzmann (pl. **Schutzleute**) m.
  policeman
Schwager,- m. brother-in-law
Schwägerin,-en f. sister-in-law
schwarz black
Schwarzbrot,-e n. pumpernickel
Schwede,-n m. Swede
Schweden n. Sweden
schweigen to be silent
Schweigen,- n. silence
Schweinebraten,- m. roast pork
Schweiz f. Switzerland
Schweizer,- m. Swiss
schwellen st.v. to swell
schwer heavy, difficult
Schwester,-n f. sister
Schwiegermutter,- f. mother-in-law
Schwiegervater,- m. father-in-law
Schwierigkeit,-en f. difficulty
schwitzen to sweat, perspire
See,-s,-n m. lake
See,- f. sea
Seefahrt,-en f. sea voyage
Seehund,-e m. sea lion
seekrank seasick
Seekrankheit f. seasickness
Seele,-n f. soul
Seeluft f. sea air
Seereise,-n f. sea trip
Segelboot,-e n. sail boat
Segen,- m. blessing
sehen st.v. to see
sehenswert remarkable
Sehenswürdigkeiten pl. sights
sehr very
Seife,-n f. soap
sein irr. st.v. to be
seit since (time)
seitdem since (time)
Seite,-n f. side, page
Selbstbildnis,-se n. self-portrait
selbstverständlich of course,
  naturally
Seligkeit f. supreme happiness,
  salvation
senden irr. w.v. to send

Sendung,-en f. shipment
Senf,-e m. mustard
September m. September
servieren to serve
Serviette,-n f. napkin
Sessel,- m. easy chair
setzen to set, put
  sich ... to sit down
sicher sure, surely
sie she, they; her, them
Sie you (pol. pl.)
Siedlung,-en f. settlement
singen st.v. to sing
Sitz,-e m. seat
sitzen st.v. to sit, fit
so so, thus
sobald as soon as
Socke,-n f. sock
sofort immediately, right away
Sohle,-n f. sole
Sohlenleder n. leather for soles
sogar even
Sohn,-e m. son
solange as long as
solch such, such a
solide substantial, conservative,
  sound
sollen ought to, shall
Sommer,- m. summer
sondern but (on the contrary)
Sonnabend,-e m. Saturday
Sonne,-n f. sun
Sonntag,-e m. Sunday
sonst otherwise, formerly
sorgen refl. v. to worry
sorglos carefree
soviel als as much as
soweit so far, that far
sowie as well as; as soon as
Spanien n. Spain
Spanier,- m. Spaniard
spät late
Spätnachmittag,-e m. late afternoon
Speck m. bacon
Speisehaus,-er n. restaurant
Speisekarte,-n f. menu
Speisesaal,-säle m. dining hall
Speisezimmer,- n. dining room
Speisewagen,- m. diner, dining car
Spiegel,- m. mirror
Spiegelei,-er n. fried egg
Spiel,-e n. game, play

spielen to play
Spinat,-e *m.* spinach
Sprache,-n *f.* language
sprechen *st.v.* to speak
Sprechstunde,-n *f.* office hour
Sprichwort,-ˉer *n.* proverb
sprichwörtlich proverbial
Spur,-en *f.* trace
Staat,-s,-en *m.* state
Staatsbürger,- *m.* citizen
Stadt,-ˉe *f.* city
städtisch municipal
stammen aus to originate from
Standuhr,-en *f.* grandfather's clock
stark strong
starten to take off, start
stattfinden *st.v.* to take place
stecken to put
stehen *st.v.* to stand, stop (watch)
stehlen *st.v.* to steal
steif stiff
Stein,-e *m.* stone
Stelle,-n *f.* place
stellen to set, put, place
Stenogramm,-e *n.* shorthand note
Stenographie,-n *f.* shorthand
stenographieren to write shorthand
Stenotypistin,-nen *f.* stenographer
sterben *st.v.* to die
stetig perpetual; steady
Steuer,- *n.* steering wheel
Stich,-e *m.* trick (card game); stitch,
  puncture
Stil,-e *m.* style
still quiet, still
stimmen to tally, be correct
  das stimmt that's correct
Stimmung,-en *f.* atmosphere, mood
Stirn,-en *f.* forehead
Stock,-ˉe *m.* flight, floor
Stockwerk,-e *n.* flight, floor
stören to disturb
stramm solid
Strasse,-n *f.* street
Strassenbahn,-en *f.* streetcar
Strecke,-n *f.* distance
strecken to stretch
Streichholz,-ˉer match
streiken to strike
strömen to stream
Strumpf,-ˉe *m.* hose, stocking

Stück,-e *n.* piece, play
studieren to study
Stuhl,-ˉe *m.* chair
Stunde,-n *f.* hour, lesson
Sturm,-ˉe *m.* storm
stürmen to rush
subtrahieren to subtract
suchen to look for, seek, search
Südamerika South America
Süddeutschland *n.* South Germany
Süden *m.* south
Summe,-n *f.* sum
sündigen to sin
Suppe,-n *f.* soup
Suppenlöffel,- *m.* table spoon
süss sweet
Sweater,- *m.* sweater

T

Tabak,-e *m.* tobacco
Tafel,-n *f.* banquet table
Tag,-e *m.* day
tagelang for days
Taille,-n *f.* waist, waistline
Tal,-ˉer *n.* valley
Tankstelle,-n *f.* gas station
Tante,-n *f.* aunt
Tanz,-ˉe *m.* dance
tanzen to dance
Tanzkunst *f.* art of dancing
Tasche,-n *f.* pocket
Taschenuhr,-en *f.* pocket watch
Tasse,-n *f.* cup
taub deaf
Taube,-n *f.* dove, pigeon
Taubheit *f.* deafness
Taxi,-s *f.* taxi
technisch technical
Tee *m.* tea
Teelöffel,- *m.* teaspoon
Teil,-e *m.* part
Teilhaber,- *m.* partner
teilnehmen *st.v.* to participate
teilweise partly
Telefon,-e *n.* telephone
telefonieren to telephone
Telefonnummer,- *f.* telephone
  number
telegrafieren to telegraph
telegrafisch by wire

Telegramm,-e n. telegram
Teller,- m. plate
Teppich,-e m. rug
teuer dear, expensive
Teufel,- m. devil
tief deep
Tiefe,-n f. depth
Tiger,- m. tiger
Tinte,-n f. ink
Tisch,-e m. table
Tischtuch,-̈er n. tablecloth
Tochter,-̈ f. daughter
Tod,-e m. death
Tomate,-n f. tomato
Tor,-e n. gate
Tor,-s,-en m. fool
töten to kill
Tracht,-en f. costume
tragen st.v. to wear, carry
Träne,-n f. tear
träumen to dream
treffen st.v. to meet
treiben st.v. to drive
trennen refl.v. to separate, part
Treppe,-n f. stairs, staircase
treten st.v. to step
Trieb,-e m. impulse, drive
trinken st.v. to drink
Trinkgeld,-er n. tip
trotz in spite of
Trumpf,-̈e m. trump
tüchtig efficient, vigorous
tun st.v. to do, make
Turm,-̈e m. tower
Turmuhr,-en f. tower clock

U

über over, above
überall everywhere
überallher from all over
Überbinger,- m. bearer
überhängen st.v. to hang over
überhaupt at all
überlassen st.v. to leave to
Übermensch,-en m. superman
übermorgen day after tomorrow
übermüden to overtire
übernachten to stay overnight
übernehmen st.v. to take over
überraschen surprise

Überraschung,-en f. surprise
übersetzen to translate
übertragen st.v. to transcribe,
  carry over
überwältigend overpowering
Uhr,-en f. watch, clock
Uhrfeder,-n f. watch spring
Uhrmacher,- m. watchmaker
Uhrmacherwerkstatt,-̈en f.
  watchmaker's workshop
Uhrwerk,-e n. the works of a watch
um around, about
um . . . zu in order to
umdrehen refl. v. to turn
umgeben st.v. surround
Umgebung,-en f. vicinity
umsehen refl.st.v. to look around,
  look back
umsonst for nothing, in vain
umstritten controversial
umwechseln to change, exchange
unangenehm unpleasant
unbedingt by all means
und and
ungefähr about, approximately
ungefährlich harmless
ungemütlich uncomfortable
ungern reluctantly, unwillingly,
  not like
Unglück,- n. misfortune, bad luck
unglücklich unhappy
Unkraut n. weeds
unmöglich impossible
unruhig restless
unschuldig innocent
unstillbar unappeasable
unten down, downstairs
unter under, below, among
unterbrechen st.v. interrupt
untergehen st.v. to perish
Untergrundbahn,-en f. subway
Unterhemd,-en n. undershirt
Unterhose,-n f. underpants
Unterkunft,-̈e f. shelter
unternehmen st.v. to undertake
Unterrock,-̈e m. slip
untersuchen to examine, investigate
Untersuchung,-en f. examination
Untertasse,-n f. saucer
unterwegs on the road
unvergesslich unforgettable

unvollendet unfinished
unzufrieden dissatisfied
Uraufführung,-en f. première
Urheimat f. original home

V

Vater,-·· m. father
Verabredung,-en f. appointment
Veränderung,-en f. alteration, charge
verbergen refl. st.v. to hide
verbinden refl. st.v. combine, connect
Verbindung,-en f. connection, fraternity
verbieten st.v. to forbid
verboten forbidden
verbringen irr. w.v. to spend
verbunden sein to be obliged
verdächtig suspicious
vereinen to unite
vereinigen to combine, unite
Vereinigten Staaten pl. United States
Vereinigung,-en f. combination
verfassen to draft
Verfassung,-en f. constitution
vergeblich in vain
vergehen st.v. to perish
vergessen st.v. to forget
vergesslich forgetful, careless
vergiessen st.v. to shed, spill
Vergnügen,- n. pleasure
Vergnügungspark,-e m. amusement park
verhaftet werden st.v. to be arrested
verheiraten to marry
Verherrlichung,-en f. glorification
verkaufen to sell
Verkehr m. traffic
verkehrt wrong
verlängern to lengthen
verlassen st.v. to leave
verlässlich dependable
verlieren st.v. to lose
verlockend tempting
verneinen to negate
verschmelzen st.v. to fuse
verschont bleiben to be spared
verschreiben st.v. to prescribe
verschweigen st.v. to keep a secret
verschwenden to waste, squander

Versprechen,- n. promise
verstauen to pack
verstehen st.v. to understand
Versuch,-e m. attempt
versuchen to try, attempt
vertonen to compose
Vertonung,-en f. composition
vertragen refl. st.v. to get along
Verwandte,-n f. & m. relative
verwenden irr. w.v. to use
verwirklichen to realize
verzeihen st.v. to forgive, excuse
verzollen to pay duty
Vetter,-s,-n m. cousin (masc.)
viel much
vielleicht perhaps
Viertel,- fourth
Vogel,-·· m. bird
Volk,-··er n. people, nation
Volkslied,-er n. folk song
volkstümlich popular
voll full
vollenden to complete
vollkommen completely
von of, from, by
vor before, in front of, ago
voraus in advance
vorbeihuschen to whiz by, fly by
vorbeikommen st.v. to pass
vorbereiten refl. w.v. to prepare
Vorbereitung,-en f. preparation
Vorderzimmer,- n. front room
vorgehen st.v. to be fast (watch), to go on
vorgestern day before yesterday
Vorhang,-··e m. drape, curtain
vorher first, previously, in advance
vorkommen st.v. to seem so, to be found
vorläufig for the present
Vormittag,-e m. forenoon
vormittags in the forenoon
vorn(e) in front
Vorname,-ns,-n m. first name
Vorort,-e m. suburb
vorschlagen st.v. to suggest
vorstellen refl.v. to introduce oneself, to imagine
Vorstellung,-en f. performance
Vortrag,-··e m. lecture
vorübergehend passing

W

Wagen,- *m.* car
wählen to elect, choose
wahr true
während while *(conj.)* during *(prep.)*
wahrscheinlich probably
Wahrzeichen,- *n.* distinctive mark
Wald,-ˮer *m.* forest, woods
Walzer,- *m.* waltz
Wanderlied,-er *n.* hiking song
wandern to hike, wander
Wanderung,-en *f.* hike
wann? when?
Ware,-en *f.* goods, commodity
Warenhaus,-ˮer *n.* department store
warten to wait
Wartesaal,-säle *m.* waiting-room (railroad)
Wartezimmer,- *n.* waiting room
warum? why?
was what, which, that
Wäsche *pl.* underwear
waschen *st.v.* to wash
Wasser,- *n.* water
Wechselgebühr,-en *f.* discount on bills
wechseln to change
Wecker,- *m.* alarm clock
weder . . . noch neither . . . nor
Weg,-e *m.* way, road, path
wegen on account of, because of
weich soft
Weihnachtszeit *f.* Christmas time
weil because
Weile,-n *f.* while
Wein,-e *m.* wine
Weisheit *f.* wisdom
weiss white
Weissbrot,-e *n.* white bread
Weisswein,-e *m.* white wine
weit far, wide
weiter further
weiterfahren *st.v.* to go on
weitergehen *st.v.* to continue, go on
Welt,-en *f.* world
Weltkrieg,-e *m.* world war
Weltstadt,-ˮe *f.* metropolis
wenig little
weniger less

wenigstens at least
wenn when, if
wer who, whoever
werden *irr. v.* to get, become
Werk,-e *n.* works
Werkstatt,-ˮen *f.* workshop
Wert,-e *m.* value, worth
Wertbrief,-e insured letter
Wertsachen *pl.* valuables
Wesen *n.* character
weshalb why
Weste,-n *f.* vest
Westen *m.* west
Wetter,- *n.* weather
wichtig important
wider against
wie how, as
wieder again
Wiederentdeckung,-en *f.* rediscovery
wiederholen to repeat
wiederkommen *st.v.* to return
wiedersehen *st.v.* to see again
wie viele? how many?
Wien Vienna
Wiener Wald *m.* Vienna Woods
wieso how, why
wieviel how much
. . . Uhr ist es? what time is it?
Wille,-ns,-n *m.* will
willkommen welcome
Wind,-e *m.* wind
winken to wave
Winter,- *m.* winter
wirklich real, really
Wirklichkeit *f.* reality
Wissen *n.* knowledge
wissen *irr.v.* to know (a fact)
wo where
Woche,-n *f.* weak
woher whence, how
wohin where to
wohl well, probably
wohnen to live, to reside
Wohnhaus,-ˮer *n.* apartment house, house
Wohnung,-en *f.* apartment
Wohnzimmer,- *n.* living room
Wolke,-n *f.* cloud
wollen to want, wish
woraufhin whereupon

Wort,-"er *n.* word
Wörterbuch,-"er *n.* dictionary
worüber what of
Wunder,- *n.* wonder
wunderbar wonderful
wünschen to wish
Wurst,-"e *f.* sausage, cold cuts
Würstchen,- *n.* sausage, frankfurter
Wurzel,-n *f.* root

Z

Zahl,-en *f.* number
zahlen to pay
zählen to count
Zahlmeister,- *m.* paymaster, purser
Zahn,-"e *m.* tooth
Zahnarzt,-"e *m.* dentist
Zahnbürste,-n *f.* toothbrush
Zahnpaste,-n *f.* toothpaste
Zahnpulver,- *n.* tooth powder
Zahnwurzel,-n *f.* root of a tooth
Zeh,-(e)s,-en *m.* toe
zeigen to show
Zeile,-n *f.* line
Zeit,-en *f.* time
Zentrum, Zentren *m.* center
zerstören to destroy
Zettel,- *m.* slip, label
Ziegel,- *m.* brick
ziehen *st.v.* to draw
ziemlich rather
Zigarette,-n *f.* cigaret
Zimmer,- *n.* room
Zitrone,-n *f.* lemon
Zitronenlimonade,-n *f.* lemonade
Zoll,-"e *m.* custom, duty

Zollamt,-"er *n.* custom-house
Zollbeamte,-n *m.* revenue officer custom
Zolldeklaration,-en *f.* customs declaration
Zollerklärung,-en *f.* customs declaration
zollfrei free of duty
zollpflichtig subject to duty
Zollrevision,-en *f.* customs examination
Zollstelle,-n *f.* custom-house
zu to (the house of)
Zucker *f.* sugar
zuerst first, at first
Zufall,-"e *m.* coincidence, chance
zufrieden satisfied, happy
Zug,-"e *m.* train
zugeben *st.v.* to admit
Zukunftsplan,-"e *m.* plan for the future
Zünder,- *m.* spark plug
Zunge,-n *f.* tongue
zurück back
zurückkehren to return
zurücksehen *st.v.* to look back
zurückziehen *st.v.* to retire
zusammen together
Zusammenbruch,-"e *m.* collapse
zwar to be sure
zweieinhalb two and a half
zweimal twice
zweitens secondly
Zwerg,-e *m.* dwarf
Zwiespalt,-"e *m.* conflict
zwingen *st.v.* to force
zwischen between

English-German
Dictionary

A

a ein
able, to be können
about ungefähr, um
above über, oben
    . . . it darüber
accept, to annehmen *st.v.*
accompany, to begleiten
according to nach
acquaintance Bekanntschaft,-en *f.*
act, to fungieren
actor Schauspieler,- *m.*
actress Schauspielerin,-nen *f.*
add, to aufschlagen *st.v.*; addieren, zusammenzählen
add to, to beilegen
address Adresse,-n *f.*
adjust, to ausgleichen *st.v.*
admire, to bewundern
admission ticket Eintrittskarte,-n *f.*
admit, to zugeben *st.v.*
adventure Erlebnis,-se *n.*
advise, to raten *st.v.*
affair Angelegenheit,-en *f.*
after nach, *prep.;* nachdem, *conj.*
    . . . that danach
afternoon Nachmittag,-e *m.*
    in the . . . nachmittags, am Nachmittag
afterwards nachher
again wieder
against gegen, wider
age *n.* Alter,- *n.*
agree, to einverstanden sein
air Luft *f.*
airfield Flugplatz,-¨e
airmail Luftpost *f.*
airplane Flugzeug,-e *n.*

airport Flughafen,- *m.*
alarm clock Wecker,- *m.*
alas leider
all all, alle; ganz
    . . . kinds of things allerlei
alley Gässchen,- *n.*
almost beinah (e), fast
alone allein
along entlang
Alps Alpen *f.*
already bereits, schon
also auch, ebenfalls
alteration Veränderung,-en *f.*
although obgleich
always immer
ambulance Krankenwagen,- *m.*
America Amerika *n.*
American Amerikaner,- *m.;* amerikanisch *adj.*
amount Betrag,-¨e *m.*
amuse oneself, to sich amüsieren
amusement park Vergnügungspark,-e *m.*
and und
angel Engel,- *m.*
angry, to be böse sein
another (one) noch ein(e)
antagonism Gegensatz,-¨e *m.*
any etwas
any time jederzeit
anymore nicht mehr
apartment Wohnung,-en *f.*
apartment house Wohnhaus,-¨er *n.*, Mietshaus,-¨er *n.*
apothecary Apotheke,-n *f.*
apparatus Apparat,-e *m.*
appear, to scheinen, *st.v.*, erscheinen, *st.v.*, aussehen, *st.v.*
apple Apfel,-¨ *m.*

apple cake Apfelkuchen,- *m.*
applesauce Apfelmus, *n.*
appointment Verabredung,-en *f.*
approach, to nähern *refl. v.*
approximately ungefähr
April April,-e *m.*
architecture Bauart,-en *f.*,
  Baukunst *f.*
arm Arm,-e *m.*
around um
arrested, to be verhaftet werden
  st.v.
arrival Ankunft,-¨e *f.*
arrive, to anlangen
art Kunst,-¨e *f.*
article Artikel,- *m.*
artist Künstler,- *m.*
artistic Künstlerisch
as wie
ask, to fragen
ask for, to bitten um, *st.v.*
asleep, to fall einschlafen *st.v.*
assume, to annehmen *st.v.*
at an, um (time)
attempt Versuch,-e *m.*
attend, to beiwohnen
attend to, to besorgen
August August *m.*
aunt Tante,-n *f.*
Austria Österreich *n.*
Austrian Österreicher,- *m.*
au revoir auf Wiedersehen
automobile Automobil,-e *n.;*
  Auto,-s *n.;* Kraftwagen,- *m.*
auto trip Autotour,-en *f.*
avenue Allee,-n *f.*
awe Scheu *f.*

B

back Rücken,- *m.,*
  zurück, *adv.*
  at the . . . hinten
bacon Speck *m.*
bad schlimm, schlecht
bad luck Unglück *n.*
baggage Gepäck,-e *n.*
baggage compartment
  Kofferraum,-¨e *m.*
baggage label Gepäckzettel,- *m.*
balcony Balkon,-e, *or,* -s *m.*

band (of musicians)
  Kapelle,-n *f.*
bank Bank,-en *f.*
banquet table Tafel,-n *f.*
barber Barbier,-e *m.*
barber shop Barbiergeschäft,-e *n.;*
  Barbierladen,- *m.*
basket Korb,-¨e *m.*
bath towel Badetuch,-¨er *n.*
bathroom Badezimmer,- *n.*
Bavaria Bayern
Bavarian bayrisch
be, to sein, *irr.v.;* befinden
  refl. st.v.
bean Bohne,-n *f.*
bear Bär,-en *m.*
bearer Überbringer,- *m.*
beat, to schlagen
beautiful schön
beauty Schönheit,-en *f.*
because weil, denn
because of wegen
become, to werden *irr. v.*
bed Bett,-en *n.*
bedroom Schlafzimmer,- *n.*
beer Bier,-e *n.*
before bevor *conj.;* vor *prep.*
beg, to bitten *st.v.*
begin, to anfangen *st.v.;*
  beginnen *st.v.*
beginning Anfang,-¨e *m.*
behind hinten, hinter
believe, to glauben
below unter
beside(s) ausser, ausserdem
better besser
between zwischen
beverage Getränk,-e *n.*
bill Rechnung,-en *f.;* Schein,-e *m.*
  (money)
bird Vogel,-¨ *m.*
birth Geburt,-en *f.*
bitter bitter
black schwarz
blank Formular,-e *n.*
bleach, to bleichen *st.v.*
bleak kahl
blessing Segen,- *m.*
blotter Löschblatt,-¨er *n.*
blouse Bluse,-n *f.*

blue blau
board Brett,-er *n.*
boil, to kochen
border Grenze,-n *f.*
born geboren
both beide
bottle Flasche,-n *f.*
bottom Boden *m.;* Grund *m.*
  from the ... von unten
box (theater) Loge,-n *f.*
boy Junge,-n *m.;* Knabe,-n *m.*
brake Bremse,-n *f.*
branch Geschäftszweig,-e *m.;*
  Branche,-n *f.*
brassiere Büstenhalter,- *m.*
bread Brot,-e *n.*
  ... and butter Butterbrot,-e *n.*
breakfast Frühstück,-e *n.*
breathe, to atmen
brick Ziegel,- *m.*
bridge Brücke,-en *f.*
briefcase Aktentasche,-n *f.;*
  Mappe,-n *f.*
bright hell
brim Krempe,-n *f.*
bring, to bringen *irr. w.v.*
bring (with one), to mitbringen *st.v.*
broad breit
broken gebrochen, verbrochen
brother Bruder,-" *m.*
brother-in-law Schwager,-" *m.*
brown braun
brush Bürste,-n *f.*
buckle on, to festschnallen, *refl.v.*
build, to bauen
build up, to aufbauen
building Gebäude,- *n.;*
  Bau,-s,-ten *m.;* Bauwerk,-e *n.*
bulb Birne,-n *f.*
burned out ausgebrannt
bus Autobus,-se *m.;* Bus,-se *m.*
business Geschäft,-e *n.*
business trip Geschäftsreise,-n *f.*
busy besetzt
but aber, sondern
butter Butter *f.*
button Knopf,-" *m.*
buy, to kaufen
by von, bei, durch, zu
by all means unbedingt

cabaret Kleinkunstbühne,-n *f.,*
  Kabarett,-s *n.*
cabbage Kohl,- *m.*
cabin Kajüte,-n *f.,* Kabine,-n *f.*
  ... number Kabinennummer,-n *f.*
  outside ... Aussenkabine,-n *f.*
cage Käfig,-e *m.*
cake Kuchen,- *m.*
calamity Jammer *m.*
call, to rufen *st.v.,* nennen *irr.w.v.*
  to ... for abholen
  to ... up anrufen *st.v.*
called, to be heissen *st.v.*
calm ruhig
camel Kamel,-e *n.*
can können
capital Hauptstadt,-"e *f.*
car Wagen,- *m.*
card Karte,-n *f.*
carefree sorglos
careful, to be hüten *refl. v.*
careless vergesslich
carp Karpfen,- *m.*
carrot Karotte,-n *f.*
carry, to tragen *st.v.,* führen
  (a store)
carry over, to übertragen *st.v.*
carton of cigarets Karton
  Zigaretten
case Fall,-"e *n.*
  in any ... jedenfalls
  in ... falls
castle Schloss,-"er *n.*
cat Katze,-n *f.*
catch up on, to nachholen
cauliflower Blumenkohl,-e *m.*
cause, to bereiten, versuchen
center, Mittelpunkt,-e *m.;*
  Zentrum, Zentren *n.*
Central Germany Mitteldeutschland *n.*
century Jahrhundert,-e *n.*
certain gewiss
chair Stuhl,-"e *m.*
  deck ... Liegestuhl,-" *m.*
  easy ... Sessel,- *m.*
chance Zufall,-"e *m.*
change Veränderung,-en *f.*
change, to wechseln
change for, to umwechseln

character Wesen,-n, Charakter,- *m.*
charm Reiz,-e *m.*
charming liebenswürdig, reizend
chat, to plaudern
cheap billig, preiswert
check Scheck,-s *m.,*
check, to nachsehen, *st.v.*
   . . . **the luggage, to** das Gepäck aufgeben
   . . . **in, to** absteigen *st.v.* (hotel)
cheek Backe,-n *f.*
cheerful fröhlich
cheerfulness Fröhlichkeit *f.*
cheese Käse,- *m.*
chicken Huhn,-¨er *n.*
   . . . **fricassee** Frikassee von Huhn *n.*
   . . . **soup** Hühnersuppe,-n *f.*
   roast . . . gebratene Huhn,-¨er *n.*
child Kind,-er *n.*
childhood Kindheit,-en *f.*
chimney Schornstein,-e *m.*
china Porzellan,-e *n.*
chocolate Schokolade *f.*
choose, to wählen
Christmas time Weihnachtszeit *f.*
church Kirche,-n *f.*
cigaret Zigarette,-n *f.*
citizen Staatsbürger,- *m.*
city Stadt,-¨e *f.*
   commercial . . . Handelsstadt,-¨e *f.*
city hall Rathaus,-¨er *n.*
class Klasse,-n *f.*
clean rein
clean, to reinigen
clock Uhr,-en *f.*
   tower . . . Turmuhr,-en *f.*
closet Schrank,-¨ *m.*
clothes Kleidung,-en *f.*
   used . . . getragene Sachen
cloud Wolke,-n *f.*
   be cloudy, to bewölkt sein
clutch Kupplung,-en *f.*
coarse derb
coat Mantel,-¨ *m.*
cobblestone Pflasterstein,-e *m.*
coffee Kaffee *m.*
coincidence Zufall,-¨e *m.*
cold cuts Wurst,-¨e *f.*
collapse Zusammenbruch,-¨e *m.*
collar Kragen,- *m.*
color Farbe,-n *f.*

comb Kamm,-¨e *m.*
comb, to kämmen
combination Vereinigung,-en *f.*
combine, to verbinden *st.v.*
come, to kommen *st.v.*
   . . . **close, to** nahekommen *st.v.*
   . . . **off, to** losgehen *st.v.*
   . . . **out, to** herauskommen *st.v.*
come in! herein!
comfort Bequemlichkeit,-en *f.*
comfortable bequem, gemütlich
commodity Artikel,- *m.*
common, in gemeinsam
company (commercial) Gesellschaft,-en *f.*
compassion Mitleid *n.*
compartment Abteil,-e *n.*
complain, to klagen
complete ganz
complete, to vollenden
completely vollkommen
compose, to vertonen, komponieren
composer Komponist,-en *m.*
composition Vertonung,-en *f.*
confess, to gestehen *st.v.*
conflict Zwiespalt,-¨e *m.*
congratulate, to gratulieren
connect, to verbinden *st.v.*
connection Verbindung,-en *f.,* Leitung,-en *f.* (telephone)
conquer, to erobern
conservative solide
construct, to anlegen
content zufrieden
   to be . . . **with** begnügen mit *refl. v.*
continue, to weitergehen *st.v.,* fortfahren *st.v.*
contribute, to beitragen *st.v.,* mitwirken
controversial umstritten
cook, to kochen
cookie Keks,-e *m.*
cordial herzlich
cordial Likör,-e *m.*
corner Ecke,-n *f.*
correct richtig
correct, to be stimmen
correspondence Korrespondenz *f.*
cost, to kosten
costume Tracht,-en *f.*
country Land, -¨er *n.*

couple Paar,-e *n.*
course Gang,-ᵉe *m.*
cousin Kusin,-s *m.*, Kusine,-n *f.*
 Vetter,-s,-n *m.*
cover, to bedecken
cow Kuh,-ᵉe *f.*
cozy gemütlich
cream Sahne *f.*
create, to schaffen *st.v.*
cross, to kreuzen
crowded besetzt, voll
crown (of head) Scheitel,- *m.*
cuff Manschette,-n *f.*
culture Kultur,-en *f.*
cup Tasse,-n *f.*
curse Fluch,-ᵉe *m.*
curtain Gardine,-n *f.*
custom (usage) Gebrauch,-ᵉe *m.*
custom-house Zollamt,-ᵉer *n.*,
 Zollstelle,-n *f.*
customs Zoll,-ᵉe *m.*
 ... declaration Zolldeklaration,-en *f.*
 ... examination Zollrevision,-en *f.*
cut, to schneiden *st.v.*
cute niedlich

D

dance *n.* Tanz,-ᵉe *m.*
dance, to tanzen
danger Gefahr,-en *f.*
dark dunkel
date Datum, Daten *n.*
daughter Tochter,-ᵉ *f.*
day Tag,-e *m.*
 days, for tagelang
deaf taub
deafness Taubheit *f.*
dealer Händler,- *m.*
dear teuer
death Tod *m.*
December Dezember *m.*
deck Deck,-e *m.*
deduction Abzug,-ᵉe *m.*
deep tief
defeat Niederlage,-n *f.*
definite bestimmt
deliverance Erlösung *f.*
den (room) Herrenzimmer,- *n.*
dentist Zahnarzt,-ᵉe *m.*
depart, to abfahren *st.v.*

department Abteilung,-en *f.*
department store Warenhaus,-ᵉer *n.*
departure Abfahrt,-en *f.*
dependable verlässlich, zuverlässig
deposit Handgeld,-er *n.*
depth Tiefe,-n *f.*
desire Lust,-ᵉe *f.*
desk Schreibpult,-e *n.*
dessert Nachtische,-e *m.*
destroy, to zerstören
develop, to entwickeln
devil Teufel,- *m.*
dictate, to diktieren
dictionary Wörterbuch,-ᵉer *n.*
die, to sterben *st.v.*
different anders
difficult schwer
difficulty Schwierigkeit,-en *f.*
dig, to graben *st.v.*
diner (car) Speisewagen,- *m.*
dining hall Speisesaal,-säle *m.*
dining room Speisezimmer,- *n.*,
 Esszimmer,- *n.*
dinner Mittagessen *n.*
directly gleich
dirty schmutzig
discount Abzug,-ᵉ *m.*
 ... on bills Wechselgebühr,-en *f.*
dish Gang,-ᵉe *m.*
dissatisfied unzufrieden
dissolve, to auflösen
distance Strecke,-n *f.*, Ferne,-n *f.*
distress Not *f.*
disturb, to stören
ditch Graben,-ᵉ *m.*
divine göttlich
do, to machen, tun *st.v.*
dog Hund,-e *m.*
dot Punkt,-e *m.*
dove Taube,-n *f.*
down unten
downstairs unten
 to go ... nach unten (gehen)
downward hinunter
drape Vorhang,-ᵉe *m.*
draw, to ziehen *st.v.*
drawer Schublade,-n *f.*
dream Traum,-ᵉe *m.*
dream, to träumen
dress Kleid,-er *n.*
dress, to anziehen *st.v.*

dresser Kommode,-n *f.*
dressing table Frisiertoilette,-n *f.*
drink, to trinken *st.v.*
drive, to treiben *st.v.*
driver Fahrer,- *m.*
druggist Drogist,-en *m.*
drugstore Apotheke,-n *f.*
during während
dwarf Zwerg,-e *m.*
dye, to färben

E

each (one) jeder
eagle Adler,- *m.*
ear Ohr,-s,-en *n.*
early früh
earnest ernst
east Osten *m.*
easy leicht
eat, to essen *st.v.*
eating Essen *n.*
eating house Speisehaus,-"er
efficient tüchtig
egg Ei,-er *n.*
  fried ... Spiegelei,-er *n.*
  scrambled ... Rührei,-er *n.*
either ... or entweder ... oder
elect, to wählen
electric light elektrisches Licht
elephant Elefant,-en *m.*
elevated railroad Hochbahn,-en *f.*
elevator Fahrstuhl,-" *m.*
emigrant Auswanderer,- *m.*
emperor Kaiser,- *m.*
empire Reich,-e *n.*
enchant, to bezaubern
enclose, to beilegen
encourage, to ermuntern
end Ende,-s,-n *n.*
end, to enden
England England *n.*
Englishman Engländer,- *m.*
engraver Kupferstecher,- *m.*
enjoy, to geniessen *st.v.*
enormous riesig
enough genug
enter, to eintreten *st.v.*
entire ganz
entrance Eingang,-"e *m.*,
  Eintritt,-e *m.*

entrust oneself, to anvertrauen
  refl. v.
envelope Kuvert,-s *n.*, Briefumschlag,-"e *m.*
equality Gleichberechtigung *f.*
especially besonders
Europe Europa *n.*
even sogar
evening Abend,-e *m.*
  in the ... abends, am Abend
everywhere überall
everything alles
evil Böse *n.*
exactly gerade
examine, to untersuchen
examination Examen,- *n.*,
  Untersuchung,-en *f.* (medical)
excellent ausgezeichnet
except ausser
exchange, to austauschen
excited aufgeregt
excuse, to entschuldigen,
  verzeihen *st.v.*
exert, to ausüben
exhausted erschöpft
exist, to bestehen *st.v.*, existieren
exit Ausgang,-" *m.*
expect, to erwarten
expensive teuer
experience, to erfahren *st.v.*,
  erleben
experienced erfahren
explain, to erklären
explanation Erklärung,-en *f.*
export Ausfuhr,-en *f.*
export, to exportieren
express train Schnellzug,-"e *m.*,
  D-Zug,-"e (Durchgangszug) *m.*
expression Ausdruck,-"e *m.*
extraordinary ausserordentlich
eye Auge,-s,-n *n.*
eyebrow Augenbraue,-n *f.*

F

face Gesicht,-e *n.*
fall (season) Herbst,-e *m.*
fall, to fallen
  to ... apart auseinanderfallen
    st.v.
  to ... out herausfallen

false falsch
familiar bekannt
famous berühmt
far weit, fern
farmer Bauer,-s,-n *m.*
fast schnell
  to be . . . (watch) vorgehen
fasten, to festschnallen, *refl. v.*
fate Schicksal,-e *n.*
father Vater,-¨ *m.*
father-in-law Schwiegervater,-¨ *m.*
fear Angst,-¨e *f.*
fear, to fürchten
feather Feder,-n *f.*
feature Gepräge,- *n.*
February Februar,-e *m.*
fee Gebühr,-en *f.*, Honorar,-e *n.*
  (physician's)
feel, to fühlen, empfinden *st.v.*,
  sich fühlen
fellow Kerl,-e *m.*
ferris wheel Riesenrad,-¨er *n.*
festival Festspiel,-e *n.*
fever Fieber *n.*
few, a few einige, ein paar
fight, to kämpfen
figure Figur,-en *f.*, Zahl,-en *f.*,
  Gestalt,-en *f.*
figure, to rechnen
fill, to füllen
fill (tooth), to plombieren,
  füllen, erfüllen
fill out, to ausfüllen
fill up, to auffüllen
filling (tooth) Plombe,-n *f.*
film Film,-e *m.*
finally endlich, schliesslich
find, to finden *st.v.*
finger Finger,- *m.*
finished fertig
fire Feuer *n.*
firm Firma, Firmen *f.*
  commercial . . . Geschäftshaus,
  -¨er *n.*
first, at first zuerst, erst, vorher
firstly erstens
first name Vorname,-ns,-n *m.*
fish Fisch,-e *m.*
fishing village Fischerdorf,-¨er *n.*
fit, to passen, sitzen, *st.v.*
flat tire Panne,-n *f.*

flee, to fliehen *st.v.*
flesh Fleisch *n.*
flight (stairs) Stock,-¨ *m.*,
  Stockwerk,-e *n.*
flight ticket Flugkarten,- *f.*
floor Stock,-¨ *m.*, Stockwerk,-e *n.*,
  Korridor,-e *m.*
flounder Flunder,-n *f.*
flower Blume,-n *f.*
folk song Volkslied,-er *n.*
follow, to folgen
food Essen *n.*
fool Narr,-en *m.*, Tor,-en *m.*
foot Fuss,-¨e *m.*
for für *prep.*, denn *conj.*
forbid, to verbieten *st.v.*
forbidden verboten
force, to zwingen *st.v.*
forehead Stirn,-en *f.*
foreign language Fremdsprache,-n
  f.
foreigner Ausländer,- *m.*,
  Ausländerin,-nen *f.*
forenoon Vormittag *m.*
  in the . . . vormittags, am Vormittag
forest Wald,-¨er *m.*
forget, to vergessen *st.v.*
forgetful vergesslich
forgive, to verzeihen *st.v.*
fork Gabel,-n *f.*
forks and spoons Bestecke *pl.*
form Form,-en *f.*, Formular,-e *n.*
formal förmlich
formerly sonst, früher
fortification Befestigung,-en *f.*
fortified befestigt
fortress Festung,-en *f.*
fortunate glücklich
fortunately glücklicherweise
founder Gründer,- *m.*
fountain Brunnen,- *m.*
fountain pen Füllfeder,- *f.*
fourth, a ein Viertel
France Frankreich *n.*
fraternity Verbindung,-en *f.*,
  Brüderlichkeit *f.*
free frei
free of charge gratis
free of customs duty zollfrei
freight Fracht,-en *f.*

freighter Frachtdampfer,- m.,
  Frachtschiff,-e n.
Frenchman Franzose,-n m.
fresh frisch
Friday Freitag,-e m.
friend Freund,-e m.,
  Freundin,-nen f.
friendly freundlich
friendship Freundschaft,-en f.
frightened, to be erschrecken st.v.
from von, aus
from all over überallher
from it davon
front, in vorn(e)
front of, in vor
fruit Obst n.
  stewed . . . Kompott,-e n.
fulfill, to erfüllen
full voll
function, to funktionieren
furnish, to möblieren
furnished möbliert
furniture Möbel pl.
further weiter
fuse, to verschmelzen st.v.
future Zukunft,- f.

G

gable Giebel,- m.
game Spiel,-e n.
garden Garten,-" m.
gasoline Benzin n.
  . . . tank Benzintank,-e m.
gas station Tankstelle,-n f.
gate Tor,-e n.
gather, to sammeln
gay lustig
gear Gang,-"e
gender Geschlecht,-er n.
general allgemein
generator Lichtmaschine,-n f.
gentleman Herr,-en m.
German Deutsche m. & f.
Germany Deutschland n.
get, to besorgen, werden, irr.v.,
  bekommen st.v.
get along, to vertragen refl. st.v.
get dressed, to sich anziehen
get in, to hereinbekommen st.v.,
  einsteigen st.v.

get off, to aussteigen st.v.
get rid of, to loswerden st.v.
get up, to aufstehen st.v.
giant Riese,-n m.
girdle Korsett,-e n.
girl Mädchen,- n.
give, to geben st.v.
give advice, to beraten st.v.
give change, to herausgeben
give in exchange, to einwechseln
give up, to herausgeben
give a message, to bestellen
glad froh
glad, to be sich freuen
gladly gern
glamour Schimmer,- m.
glass Glas,-"er n.
glassware Glaswaren pl.
glorification Verherrlichung,-en f.
glove Handschuh,-e m.
go, to gehen st.v.
  to . . . down hinuntergehen st.v.
  to . . . on passieren, vorgehen,
    st.v., weitergehen, st.v.,
    weiterfahren, st.v.
good gut
good fellowship Brüderschaft,-en f.
goods Ware,-en f.
gradually allmählich
grand grossartig
grandfather Grossvater,-" m.
grandfather's clock Standuhr,-en f.
grandmother Grossmutter,-" f.
grandson Enkel,- m.
grapefruit Pompelmus,-e f.
grateful dankbar
gray grau
grease, to ölen
great gross
greed Gier f.
green grün
greet, to grüssen
ground floor Erdgeschoss,-e n.
grown-up erwachsen
guess, to raten st.v.
guest Gast,-" m.
guest room Fremdenzimmer,- n.
guidance Führung,-en f.
gum Gaumen,- m.

H

hair Haar,-e n.
hair oil Haaröl,-e n.
hair tonic Haarwasser,- n.
hairdresser Friseur,-e m.,
Friseuse,-n f.
hairdressing salon Frisiersalon,-s m.
half halb
a . . . ein Halbes
the . . . die Hälfte
hall Saal, Säle m., Korridor,-e m.
ham Schinken m.
hang over, to überhängen st.v.
hang up, to aufhängen st.v.
happen, to passieren, geschehen st.v.
happiness Glück n.
happy glücklich, zufrieden,
froh, fröhlich
happy-go-lucky leichtlebig
harbor Hafen,-¨ m.
hard hart
hardly kaum
harmless ungefährlich
hat Hut,-¨e m.
felt . . . Filzhut,-¨ m.
have, to haben irr.v.
he er
head Kopf,-¨e m.
headache Kopfschmerz,-es,-en m.
hear, to hören
heart Herz,-ens, en n.
heartily herzlich
heaven Himmel,- m.
heavy schwer, derb
height Höhe,-n f.
help Hilfe,-n f.
help, to helfen st.v.
hem Saum,-¨e m.
here hier
. . . (direction to place) hierher
hide, to verbergen refl., st.v.
high hoch
highway Autobahn,-¨en f.
hike Wanderung,-en f.
hike, to wandern
historical geschichtlich
history Geschichte f.
hold, to halten st.v.
hole Loch,-¨er n.
holy heilig
homesickness Heimweh n.

hope, to hoffen
hope, I (it is to be hoped)
hoffentlich
horrified entsetzt
horse Pferd,-e n.
hose Strumpf,-¨e m.
hospital Krankenhaus,-¨er n.
hotel Hotel,-s,-s n.
. . . lobby Hotelhalle,-n f.
hour Stunde,-n f.
house Haus,-¨er n.
at the . . . of bei
one-family . . .
Einfamilienhaus,-¨er n.
housewife Hausfrau,-en f.
how wie, wieso, woher
how many? wie viele?
human being Mensch,-en m.
hunger Hunger m.
hungry hungrig
hunt, to jagen
hurry, to beeilen refl. v.
husband Gatte,-n m.

I

ice cream Gefrorenes n.
ice water Eiswasser n.
idea Idee,-n f.
identification paper
Ausweispapier,-e n.
if wenn, ob
imagine, to vorstellen refl. v.
immediately gleich, sofort
immigrant Einwanderer,- m.
import Einfuhr,-en f.
import, to einführen
importance Bedeutung,-en f.
important wichtig
impossible unmöglich
impress, to beeindrucken
impression Eindruck,-¨e m.
impressive eindrucksvoll
impulse Trieb,-e m.
in in
in advance im voraus
inasmuch da
incline, to neigen
increase, to erhöhen
indulge, to hingeben refl. st.v.
inflammation Entzündung,-en f.
inflame, to entzünden

influence Einfluss,-"e *m.*
inform, to benachrichtigen
information Auskunft,-"e *f.*
information desk
　Auskunftsstelle,-n *f.*
inhabitant Einwohner,- *m.*
ink Tinte,-n *f.*
innocent unschuldig
insane geisteskrank
inspire, to einflössen *st.v.*
instead of anstatt
instill, to einflössen *st.v.*
instructive lehrreich
intellectual geistig
interesting interessant
interlock, to einhaken
interrupt, to unterbrechen *st.v.*
into in, hinein
introduce, to bekanntmachen,
　vorstellen, einführen
introduce oneself, to sich vorstellen
in vain vergeblich, umsonst
investigate, to untersuchen
invitation Einladung,-en *f.*
invite, to einladen *st.v.*
it es
Italian Italiener,- *m.*
Italy Italien *n.*

J

jacket Jacke,-n *f.*
jam Marmelade,-n *f.*
January Januar *m.*
jelly Gelee,-s *n.*
join, to anschliessen *refl., st.v.*
joint gemeinsam
joke, to scherzen
joy Freude,-n *f.*
jubilation Jubel *m.*
juice Saft,-"e *m.*
July Juli,- *m.*
June Juni,- *m.*
just ebenso
just now gerade
just so ebenso
just across gerade über

K

keep, to halten *st.v.*
　to ... a secret verschweigen *st.v.*
key Schlüssel,- *m.*

kill, to töten
kind freundlich
kiss Kuss,-"e *m.*
kiss, to küssen
kitchen Küche,-n *f.*
knapsack Rucksack,-"e *m.*
knife Messer,- *n.*
knight Ritter,- *m.*
knives, forks, and spoons
　Bestecke,- *pl.*
knock, to klopfen
know, to erkennen *irr. w. v.*
　to ... (a fact) wissen *irr. v.*
　to ... (a person, place)
　kennen, *irr. w. v.*
knowledge Wissen *n.*
known bekannt

L

label Zettel,- *m.*
lace, to einziehen *st.v.*
lady Dame,-n *f.*
lady's coat Damenmantel,-"
lake See,-n *m.*
lamb chop Hammelkotelett,-s *n.*
lamb, leg of Hammelkeule,-n *f.*
lamp Lampe,-n *f.*
land, to landen
landscape Landschaft,-en *f.*
language Sprache,-n *f.*
large gross
last letzt
　... at endlich
last, to dauern
late spät
latest thing Neuste *n.*
laugh, to lachen
laughter Gelächter,- *n.*
lay, to legen
lead, to führen
learn, to lernen
least, at wenigstens
leather Leder *n.*
leather goods Lederwaren *pl.*
leave, to verlassen *st.v.*,
　überlassen *st.v.*
lecture Vortrag,-"e *m.*
left links
leg Bein,-e *n.*
lemon Zitrone,-n *f.*
lemonade Zitronen Limonade,-n *f.*

length Länge,-n f.
lengthen, to verlängern
less weniger
lesson Stunde,-n f.
let lassen st.v.
letter Brief,-e m.
  insured ... Wertbrief,-e m.
  air mail ... Luftpostbrief,-e m
  registered ...
    Einschreibebrief,-e m.
  ... of recommendation
    Empfehlungsbrief,-e m.
lettuce grüner Salat
lie, to liegen st.v.
light hell, leicht
light Licht,-e n.
light, to leuchten
lighten, to blitzen
lighter (cigarette) Feuerzeug,-e n.
lightning Blitz m.
like wie (prep.)
like gern
like, to gefallen, st.v., mögen
limb Glied,-er n.
limited begrenzt
line Leitung,-en f., Zeile,-n f.
liner, ocean Ozeandampfer,- m.
lion Löwe,-n m.
listen, to hören
little klein, gering
little, a etwas, ein bisschen, wenig
little matter Kleinigkeit,-en f.
live, to leben (exist); wohnen
  (reside)
lively lebhaft, munter
  calf's ... Kalbsleber f.
living room Wohnzimmer,- n.
local train Personenzug,-"e m.
long lang
  as ... as solange
look, to aussehen st.v.
look after, to aufpassen
look around, to sich umsehen st.v.
look back, to zurücksehen st.v.
look up, to aufsuchen
lose, to verlieren st.v.
love Liebe f.
love, to lieben
lovely nett, lieblich
low (tire) schlapp
luggage Gepäck,-e n.

... office Gepäckannahme,-n f.
... rack Gepäcknetz,-e n.
lung Lunge,-n f.

M

main road Hauptverkehrsstrasse,-n f.
main street Hauptstrasse,-n f.
make, to machen, schaffen st.v.,
  tun, st.v.
man Mann,-"er m.
management Leitung,-en f.
manicure Maniküre,-n f.
many viel
many a mancher
map Landkarte,-n f.
March März,-e m.
mark Mark f.
marmalade Marmelade,-n f.
marry, to heiraten, verheiraten
  refl.v.
masculine männlich
master Herr,-en m.
masterpiece Meisterwerk,-e n.
match Streichholz,-"er n.
matter Angelegenheit,-en f.
  ... of taste Geschmacksache,-n f.
may mögen, dürfen
May Mai,-e m.
meal Essen,- n., Mahlzeit,-en f.
means Mittel,-n n.
  by all ... jedenfalls
mean, to meinen, bedeuten
meantime, in the inzwischen
measure, to messen
meat Fleisch n.
meat broth Fleischbrühe,-n f.
mechanic Mechaniker,- m.
medicine Medizin,-en f.
meet, to kennenlernen, treffen
menu Speisekarte,-n f.
merry fröhlich
metropolis Grosstadt,-"e f.,
  Weltstadt,-"e f.
midday Mittag,-e m.
middle Mitte,- n.
Middle Ages Mittelalter n.
middleman Mittler,- m.,
  Mittlerin,-nen f.
midnight Mitternacht,-"e f.
mighty mächtig
mile Meile,-n f.

milk Milch *f.*
minute Minute,-n *f.*
mirror Spiegel,- *m.*
misfortune Unglück,- *m.*
miss, to fehlen
Mister Herr,-en *m.*
misunderstanding
  Missverständnis,-se *n.*
modern times Neuzeit *f.*
moment Augenblick,-e *m.*,
  Moment,-e *m.*
Monday Montag,-e *m.*
money Geld *n.*
monkey Affe,-n *m.*
month Monat,-e *m.*
monument Denkmal,-"er *n.*
mood Stimmung,-en *f.*
more mehr
  ... **than** mehr als
morning Morgen,- *m.*
  in the ... morgens, am Morgen
mostly meistens
mother Mutter,-" *f.*
mother-in-law Schwiegermutter,-" *f.*
motion Bewegung,-en *f.*
motorboat Motorboot,-e
motorcycle Motorrad,-"er *n.*
mountain Berg,-e *n.*
mountain lake Bergsee,-n *m.*
mountain top Gipfel,- *m.*
mouse Maus,-"e *f.*
mouth Mund,-"er *m.*
mouth wash Mundwasser,- *n.*
movies Kino,-s *n.*
Mrs. Frau,-en *f.*
much viel
  as ... **as** soviel als
  how ... wieviel
multiply, to multiplizieren
municipal städtisch
muscle Muskel,-n *f.*
music Musik *f.*
must müssen
mustard Mostrich *m.*, Senf *m.*
mutual gegenseitig

N

nail Nagel,-" *m.*
  ... **polish** Nagelpolitur,-en *f.*
  ... **scissors** Nagelschere,-n *f.*
name Name,-ns,-n *m.*

named, to be heissen *st.v.*
napkin Serviette,-n *f.*
narrow eng
nation Volk,-"er *n.*, Nation,-en *f.*
native country Heimat,-en *f.*
naturally selbstverständlich,
  natürlich
nature Natur *f.*
near neben, in der Nähe
nearness Nähe *f.*
necessary nötig
necessary things(s) Nötige *n.*
neck Hals,-"e *m.*, Nacken,- *m.*
necktie Schlips,-e *m.*
need, to brauchen
negate, to verneinen
neither ... **nor** weder ... noch
nephew Neffe,-n *m.*
nerve Nerv,-en *m.*
new neu
next nächst
next to neben
next door nebenan
nice nett
niece Nichte,-n *f.*
night Nacht,-"e *f.*
  at ... nachts, in der Nacht
night table Nachttisch,-e *m.*
no nein
nobody niemand
nod, to nicken
noise Geräusch,-e *n.*
noon Mittag,-e *m.*
  at ... mittags, in der Mittag
north Norden *m.*
Norway Norwegen *n.*
Norwegian Norweger,- *m.*
nose Nase,-n *f.*
not nicht
notice, to bemerken, merken
notify, to benachrichtigen
November November *m.*
now jetzt, nun
number Nummer,-n *f.*, Zahl,-en *f.*
number, to numerieren

O

oatmeal Hafergrütze *f.*
occupy, to beschäftigen
occur, to einfallen *st.v.*
October Oktober *m.*

odd eigenartig
of von
... it davon
offer, to darbieten *st.v.*, anbieten *st.v.*
office Büro,-s *n.*, Kontor,-e *n.*
office building Geschäftshaus,-"er *n.*
office hour Sprechstunde,-n *f.*
office room Büroraum,-"e *m.*
often oft
oil Öl,-e *n.*
old alt
on an, auf
once einmal
once again nochmals
one ein, eins
one and a half anderthalb, eineinhalb
only einzig, nur
open, to aufmachen
opera Oper,-n *f.*
opportunity Gelegenheit,-en *f.*
opposite geradeüber, gegenüber
or oder
orange Orange,-n *f.*
orange juice Orangensaft,-"e *m.*
order Ordnung,-en *f.*
... to be in in Ordnung sein
order, to bestellen
order to, in um ... zu
originate from, to stammen aus
other ander
otherwise sonst
ought to sollen
out aus, hinaus
... into hinaus
outside aussen
... of ausserhalb
over über
... it darüber
over there drüben
overpowering überwältigend
own eigen
owner Inhaber,- *m.*

P

pace Schritt,-e *m.*
pack, to verstauen
pack (in), to einpacken
page Seite,-n *f.*

pain Schmerz,-es,-en *m.*
paint, to malen
painter Maler *m.*
painting Gemälde,- *n.*
Malerei,-en *f.*
paintings, collection of Gemäldesammlung,-en *f.*
pair Paar,-e *n.*
pants Hose,-n *f.*
paper Papier,-e *n.*
parents Eltern *pl.*
park Park,-e *m.*
part Teil,-e *m.*
part, to sich trennen
participate teilnehmen *st.v.*
partly teilweise
partner Teilhaber,- *m.*
party Gesellschaft,-en *f.*
Partei,-en *f.*
pass, to passieren, vorbeikommen *st.v.*
... an examination ein Examen bestehen
passageway Gang,-"e *m.*
passing vorübergehend
Passion Play Passionsspiel,-e *n.*
passport Pass,-" *m.*
paste, to kleben
path Weg,-e *m.*
pay, to zahlen, bezahlen
pay attention, to aufpassen
pay duty, to verzollen
paymaster Zahlmeister,- *m.*
peach Pfirsich,-e *m.*
pear Birne,-n *f.*
pea Erbse,-n *f.*
pencil Bleistift,-e *m.*
penetrate, to eindringen *st.v.*
penny Pfennig,- *m.*
people Leute, *pl.*, Volk,-"er *n.*, Publikum *n.*
pepper Pfeffer *m.*
perceive, to erkennen *irr. w.v.*
per cent Prozent,-e *n.*
perform, to aufführen
performance Vorstellung,-en *f.*
Aufführung,-en *f.*
perhaps vielleicht
permanent wave Dauerwelle,-n *f.*
permission Erlaubnis,-se *f.*

permitted, to be dürfen
perpetual stetig
personal persönlich
perspire, to schwitzen
physician Arzt,-¨e *m.*
piano Klavier,-e *n.*
pick, to aussuchen
pick up, to aufnehmen *st.v.*,
aufheben *st.v.*
picture Bild,-er *n.*
piece Stück,-e *n.*
pigeon Taube,-n *f.*
pinch, to drücken
pink rosa
pitcher Krug,-¨ *m.*
place Stelle,-n *f.*
Ort,-e *m.*, Amt,-¨er *n.*
Platz,-¨e *m.*
... of birth Geburtsstätte,-n
place, to stellen
place oneself, to versetzen *refl. v.*
plague Pest,-en *f.*
plain einfach
perish, to vergehen *st.v.*,
untergehen *st.v.*
plan, to planen
plate Teller,- *m.*
platform Bahnsteig,-e *m.*
play Stück,-e *n.*, Spiel,-e *n.*
play, to spielen
pleasant angenehm
please bitte
pleased, to be gefallen
pleasure Vergnügen,- *n.*
plum Pflaume,-n *f.*
pocket Tasche,-n *f.*
pocket watch Taschenuhr,-en *f.*
poet Dichter,- *m.*
point Punkt,-e *m.*
Poland Polen *n.*
Pole Pole,-n *m.*
police Polizei *f.*
policeman Schutzmann (*pl.*
Schutzleute) *m.*
poor arm
popular volkstümlich
porcelain Porzellan,-e *n.*
pork Schweinefleisch *n.*
porter Gepäckträger,- *m.*
possession Besitz,-e *m.*
possibility Möglichkeit,-en *f.*

possible möglich
if ... möglichst
post card Postkarte,-n *f.*
post office Postamt,-¨er *n.*
potato Kartoffel,-n *f.*
...dumpling Kartoffelkloss,
-¨e *m.*
boiled ... Salzkartoffeln *pl.*
fried ... Bratkartoffeln *pl.*
mashed ... Kartoffelbrei *m.*
power Macht,-¨e *f.*
powerful gewaltig
praise, to loben
pray, to beten
prefer, to lieber haben, vorziehen
st.v.
première Uraufführung,-en *f.*
premonition Ahnung,-en *f.*
preparation Vorbereitung,-en *f.*
prepare, to vorbereiten *refl.v.*
prepared bereit
prescribe, to verschreiben *st.v.*
prescription Rezept,-e *n.*
present Gegenwart
for the ... vorläufig
presently bald
preserve, to erhalten *st.v.*
press, to drücken
pretty hübsch, nett
prevail, to herrschen
previously vorher
price Preis,-e *m.*
raise the ... aufschlagen *st.v.*
private office Privatkontor,-e *n.*
probably wahrscheinlich, wohl
proceed, to abspielen *refl.v.*
promenade deck Promenaden-
deck,-e *n.*
promise Versprechen,- *n.*
proverb Sprichwort,-¨er *n.*
proverbial sprichwörtlich
prune Backpflaume,-n *f.*
public öffentlich
pull in, to einziehen *st.v.*
pump up, to aufpumpen
pumpernickel Schwarzbrot,-¨e
pupil Schüler,- *m.*
purchase Einkauf,-¨e *m.*
pure rein
purser Zahlmeister,- *m.*
put, to legen, stecken, setzen, stellen

put on, to aufsetzen, anziehen *st..v*
put soles on, to besohlen

Q

quality Qualität,-en *f.*
quick schnell
quiet ruhig, still

R

radiator (car) Kühler,- *m.*
railroad Eisenbahn,-en *f.*
rain Regen,- *m.*
rain, to regnen
raincoat Regenmantel,-¨
raise, to heben *st.v.*
rampart Festungswall,-¨e *m.*
raspberry Himbeere,-n *f.*
rat Ratte,-n
rate of exchange Kurs,-e *m.*
rather lieber, eher, ziemlich
razor Rasiermesser,- *n.*
razor blade Rasierklinge,-n *f.*
reach, to erreichen, reichen
reach into, to hineinreichen
read, to lesen *st.v.*
ready bereit, fertig
real wirklich, echt
reality Wirklichkeit *f.*
realize, to verwirklichen
rear, in the hinten
rebuild, to aufbauen
rebuilding Neubau,-s,-ten *m.*
receive, to bekommen *st.v.*
recognize, to erkennen *irr. w.v.*,
    anerkennen *irr. w.v.*
recommend, to empfehlen *st.v.*
recommendation Empfehlung,-en *f.*
recreation Erholung,-en *f.*
red rot
redeem, to einlösen
rediscovery Wiederentdeckung,-en *f.*
refer to, to beziehen auf *refl.v.*
refreshing erfrischend
register, to einschreiben *st.v.*
rejoice, to freuen *refl.v.*
relate, to erzählen
relative Verwandte,-n *f. & m.*
reluctantly ungern
remain, to bleiben *st.v.*

remainder Rest,-e *m.*
remarkable sehenswert
remember, to merken *refl.v.*
remind one, to erinnern *refl.v.*
remote entfernt
rent, to mieten
repair, to reparieren
repairs Reparatur,-en *f.*
repeat, to wiederholen
report, to berichten
reputation Ruf *m.*
reserve, to reservieren
reside, to wohnen
respectfully hochachtungsvoll
rest Rast *m.*
rest, to ruhen, ausruhen
restaurant Speisehaus,-¨er *n.*,
    Gasthaus,-¨er *n.*
restless unruhig
retire, to zurückziehen *refl. st.v.*
return Rückkehr *f.*
return, to zurückkehren
revenue officer Zollbeamte,-n *m.*
rice Reis *m.*
rich reich
ride, to fahren *st.v.*
ride around, to herumfahren
right recht, rechts
right away gleich, sofort
ring Ringe,-e *m.*
ring, to klingen *st.v.*
rip, to aufreissen *st.v.*
rise, to aufstehen *st.v.*
rise up, to hinaufsteigen *st.v.*
risk, to riskieren
river Fluss,-¨e *m.*
road Weg,-e *m.*
road map Autobahnkarte,-en *f.*
roaring schallend
robust drall
roll Brötchen,- *n.*
roller coaster Berg-und
    Talbahn,-en *f.*
roof Dach,-¨er *n.*
room Zimmer,- *n.*, Raum,-¨e *m.*
    single ... Einzelzimmer,- *n.*
    back ... Hinterzimmer,- *n.*
    front ... Vorderzimmer,- *n.*
root Wurzel,-n *f.*
round rund
rowboat Ruderboot,-e *n.*

rubber Gummischuh,-e *m.*
rug Teppich,-e *m.*
run, to laufen *st.v.*
　...around herumlaufen *st.v.*
rush, to stürmen
Russia Russland *n.*
Russian Russe,-n *m.*
rye bread Roggenbrot,-e *n.*

S

sailboat Segelboot,-e *n.*
salad Salat,-e *m.*
sale Ausverkauf,-"e *m.*
salt Salz,-e *n.*
salvation Rettung,-en *f.*
same, the ebenso, dasselbe
satisfied zufrieden
satisfy, to befriedigen
Saturday Sonnabend,-e *m.*
saucer Untertasse,-n *f.*
sausage Wurst,-"e *f.*
save, to erlösen
save for, to aufsparen
say, to sagen
school Schule,-n *f.*
scold, to schelten *st.v.*
sea See,-n *f.*
sea lion Seehund,-e *m.*
seam Naht,-"e *f.*, Saum,-"e *m.*
seaport Hafenstadt,-"e *f.*
search, to suchen
seasick seekrank
seasickness Seekrankheit *f.*
seat Platz,-"e *m.*, Sitz,-e *m.*
second zweite
secondly zweitens
secret Geheimnis,-se *n.*
see, to sehen *st.v.*
see again, to wiedersehen
seek, to suchen
seek for, to aufsuchen
seem, to scheinen *st.v.*
seem to, to vorkommen *st.v.*
seemingly scheinbar
self-portrait Selbstbildnis,-se *n.*
sell, to verkaufen
send, to senden *irr.w.v.*
send regards, to grüssen
separate, to trennen *refl.v.*
September September *m.*
serious ernst

serve, to dienen, servieren
service Bedienung,-en *f.*
　Dienst,-e *m.*
set, to stellen, setzen
set upon, to aufsetzen
settlement Siedlung,-en *f.*
several verschieden, mehrere
several times ein paarmal
sew, to nähen
sex Geschlecht,-er *n.*
shade Schatten,- *m.*
shady schattig
shake off, to abschütteln
shall sollen
shape Form,-en *f.*
shaving brush Rasierpinsel,- *m.*
shaving soap Rasierseife,-n *f.*
she sie
shed, to vergiessen *st.v.*
shelter Unterkunft,-"e *f.*
site Lage,-n *f.*
shining leuchtend
ship Schiff,-e *n.*
shipment Sendung,-en *f.*
shirt Oberhemd,-en *n.*
shoe Schuh,-e *m.*
shine, to putzen
shoelace Schnürsenkel,- *m.*
shoemaker Schuhmacher,- *m.*
short kurz
shorthand Stenographie,-n *f.*
shorthand note Stenogramm,-e *n.*
shorts Unterhose,-n *f.*
shout, to rufen *st.v.*
show, to zeigen
shuffle (cards), to mischen
shutter Fensterladen,-" *m.*
sick krank
side Seite,-n *f.*
sight Anblick,-e *m.*
sights Sehenswürdigkeiten *pl.*
sign Schild,-er *m.*
significant bedeutend
silence Schweigen,- *n.*
silverware Bestecke *pl.*
similar ähnlich
simple einfach
simplicity Einfachheit *f.*
sin, to sündigen
since da (reason) *conj.*; seitdem
　(time)

sing, to singen *st.v.*
sister-in-law Schwägerin,-nen *f.*
sit, to sitzen *st.v.*
sit down, to setzen *refl.v.*
size Grösse,-n *f.*
skirt Rock,-¨e *m.*
sky Himmel,- *m.*
sleep Schlaf *m.*
sleep, to schlafen *st.v.*
sleeve Ärmel,- *m.*
slice Scheibe,-n *f.*, Schnitte,-n *f.*
slip (paper) Zettel,-*m.*
 . . . (clothing) Unterrock,-¨e *m.*
slow (watch), to be nachgehen
small klein
small change Kleingeld *n.*
smile, to lächeln
smoke, to rauchen
smoking room Rauchsalon,-s *m.*,
 Rauchzimmer,- *n.*
snake Schlange,-n *f.*
snow Schnee,- *m.*
so so
so far soweit
so that damit
soap Seife,-n *f.*
sock Socke,-n *f.*
soft weich
soiled schmutzig
sold out ausverkauft
sole Sohle,-n *f.*
some ein bisschen, etwas
son Sohn,-¨e *m.*
song Lied,-er *n.*
soon bald
 as . . . as sobald
soul Seele,-n *f.*
soup Suppe,-n *f.*
south Süden *m.*
South America Südamerika
South Germany Süddeutschland
space Raum,-¨ *m.*
Spain Spanien *n.*
Spaniard Spanier,- *m.*
spare, to verschonen
spark plug Zünder,- *m.*
speak, to sprechen *st.v.*
specialty Branche,-n *f.*, Geschäftszweig,-e *m.*
specialty Geschäftszweig,-e *m.*
spectators Publikum *n.*

spell Bann,- *m.*
spend (time), to verbringen *irr. w.v.*
spill, to vergiessen *st.v.*
spinach Spinat,-e *m.*
spirit Geist *m.*
spite of, in trotz
splendid herrlich
spoon Löffel,- *m.*
spot Ort,-e *m.*
spring Frühling,-e *m.*
spring Feder,-n *f.*
square Platz,-¨e *m.*
staircase Treppe,-n *f.*
stairs Treppe,-n *f.*
stamp Briefmarke,-n *f.*
stand, to stehen *st.v.*
start, to abfahren *st.v.*, starten,
 losfahren *st.v.*
state Staat,-s,-en *m.*
stateroom Kabine,-n *f.*, Kajüte,-n *f.*
station (railroad) Bahnhof,-¨e *m.*
stay, to bleiben *st.v.*
steal, to stehlen *st.v.*
steamer Dampfer,- *m.*
steam ticket Schiffsfahrkarte,-n *f.*
steering wheel Steuer,- *n.*
stenographer Stenotypistin,-nen *f.*
step Schritt,-e *m.*
step, to treten *st.v.*
step up to, to herantreten an *st.v.*
stick, to kleben
stiff steif
still (yet) noch, doch
stimulate, to anregen
stimulation Anregung,-en *f.*
stitch, to nähen
stocking Strumpf,-¨e *m.*
stomach Magen,- *m.*
stone Stein,-e *m.*
stop, to halten *st.v.*, haltmachen
store Laden,-¨ *m.*
storm Sturm,-¨e *m.*
story Geschichte,-n *f.*
straight ahead geradeaus
strawberry Erdbeere,-n *f.*
stream, to strömen
streetcar Strassenbahn,-en *f.*
strength Kraft,-¨e *f.*
strenuous anstrengend
street Strasse,-n *f.*
stretch, to strecken

strike, to schlagen *st.v.*, streiken
strive for, to streben nach
strong stark
stronghold Burg-en *f.*
struggle Kampf,-"e *m.*
study, to studieren
style Bauart,-en *f.*, Stil,-e *m.*
substantial solide
subtract, to abziehen *st.v.*,
  subtrahieren
suburb Vorort,-e *m.*
subway Untergrundbahn,-en *f.*
such solch
suddenly plötzlich
suffering Leiden,- *n.*
sugar Zucker *f.*
suggest, to vorschlagen *st.v.*
suit Anzug,-"e *m.*
suit, to passen
suitcase Handkoffer,- *m.*
sum Betrag,-"e *m.*, Summe,-n *f.*
summer Sommer,- *m.*
sun Sonne,-n *f.*
Sunday Sonntag,-e *m.*
supper Abendmahl,-e *n.*,
  Abendessen *n.*
sure sicher
surprise Überraschung,-en *f.*
surpise, to überraschen
surround, to umgeben *st.v.*
suspicious verdächtig
sweat, to schwitzen
sweater Sweater,- *m.*
Swede Schwede,-n *m.*
Sweden Schweden *n.*
sweet süss
swell, to schwellen *st.v.*
switch Schalter,- *m.*
switch on, to einschalten
switch off, to ausschalten
Swiss Schweizer,- *m.*
Switzerland Schweiz *f.*
synchronize, to synchronisieren

T

table Tisch,-e *m.*
tablecloth Tischtuch,-"er *n.*
tablespoon Suppenlöffel,- *m.*
tail light Rücklicht,-er *n.*
take, to nehmen *st.*
take care of, to erledigen

take a rest, to sich ausruhen
take in, to aufnehmen *st.v.*
take off, to abziehen *st.v.*, starten
take out, to herausnehmen *st.v.*
take over, to übernehmen *st.v.*
take place, to stattfinden *st.v.*
tally, to stimmen
taste Geschmack,-"e *m.*
taste, to schmecken
taxi Autodroschke,-n *f.*, Taxi,-s *f.*
tea Tee *m.*
teacher Lehrer,- *m.*
tear Träne,-n *f.*
tear, to reissen *st.v.*
tear open, to aufreissen *st.v.*
tease, to necken
teaspoon Teelöffel,- *m.*
technical technisch
telegram Telegramm,-e *n.*
telegraph, to telegrafieren
telephone Telefon,-e *n.*
  Fernsprecher,- *m.*
telephone book Telefonbuch,-"er *n.*
telephone number
  Telefonnummer,- *n.*
telephone, to telefonieren,
  anrufen *st.v.*
tell, to erzählen, sagen
temple Schläfe,-n *f.*
tempting verlockend
than als
thank, to danken
thanks, thank you danke
that das *dem. or rel. pron.;* das *conj.*
that is das heisst(*d.h.*)
that much so viel
that one jener
the der, die, das
the . . .the je . . . desto
then dann
there da, dort
therefore darum
thing Sache,-n *f.*, Ding,-en *n.*
think, to denken *irr.w.v.*, glauben
third dritte
third, a ein Drittel
this dies
this one dieser
thorough gründlich
three drei
three times dreimal

throat Hals,-̈e *m.*
through durch
thunder Donner,- *m.*
thunderstorm Gewitter,- *n.*
Thursday Donnerstag,-e *m.*
ticket Karte,-n *f.*, Eintrittskarte,-n *f.*, Fahrkarte,-n *f.*
ticket window Schalter,- *m.*
tiger Tiger,- *m.*
tight eng
tighten (a screw), to anziehen *st.v.*
till bis
time Zeit,-en *f.*, Mal,-e *n.*
   at that ... damals
   for the ... being vorläufig
timetable Fahrplan,-̈e *m.*
tip Trinkgeld,-er *n.*
tire Reifen,- *m.*
tired müde
to zu, nach, bis, an
tobacco Tabak,-e *m.*
today heute
today's heutig
toe Zeh,-es,-en *m.*
together zusammen
tomato Tomate,-n *f.*
tomorrow morgen
   day after ... übermorgen
tongue Zunge,-n *f.*
too auch
tooth Zahn,-̈e *m.*
toothbrush Zahnbürste,-n *f.*
toothpaste Zahnpaste,-n *f.*
tooth powder Zahnpulver,- *n.*
touching rührend
tourism Fremdenverkehr, *m.*
tourist trade Fremdenverkehr, *m.*
toward gegen
towel (hand) Handtuch,-̈er *n.*
tower Turm,-̈e *m.*
trace Spur,-en *f.*
traffic Verkehr *m.*
train Zug,-̈e *m.*
   express ... Schnellzug,-̈e *m.*
training Ausbildung *f.*
transcribe, to übertragen *st.v.*
travel, to reisen, fahren *st.v.*
travel bureau Reisebüro,-s *n.*
travelers' check Reisescheck,-s *m.*
traveling bag Reisetasche,-n *f.*
traveling companion
   Reisegefährte,-n *m.*

traveling experience
   Reiseerlebnis,-se *n.*
tree Baum,-̈e *m.*
tributary Nebenfluss,-̈e *m.*
trick (card game) Stich,-e *m.*
trip Reise,-n *f.*, Fahrt,-en *f.*
trousers Hose,-n *f.*
trout Forelle,-n *f.*
true wahr
truly yours hochachtungsvoll
trump Trumpf,-̈e *m.*
trunk Koffer,- *m.*
try, to versuchen
try out, to ausprobieren
Tuesday Dienstag,-e *m.*
turn (road) Biegung,-en *f.*
turn, to umdrehen *refl.v.*
turn into, to einbiegen *st.v.*
turn off, to ausschalten
turn on, to einschalten
twice zweimal
two zwei
two and a half zweieinhalb
type Art,-en *f.*
typewriter Schreibmaschine,-n *f.*

U

ugly hässlich
umbrella Regenschirm,-e *m.*
uncle Onkel,- *m.*
uncomfortable ungemütlich
under unter
undershirt Unterhemd,-en *n.*
understand, to erkennen *irr.w.v.*, verstehen, *st.v.*
undertake, to unternehmen *st.v.*
understanding Erkenntnis,-se *f.*
underwear Wäsche, Unterwäsche *pl.*
uneven holprig
unfinished unvollendet
unforgettable unvergesslich
unfortunately leider
unhappy unglücklich
unique einzigartig
unit Einheit,-en *f.*
unite, to vereinen
United States Vereinigten Staaten *pl.*
unlock, to aufschliessen *st.v.*
unmarried ledig
unpack, to auspacken

unpleasant unangenehm
until bis
unwillingly ungern
up oben,auf
up to now bisher
upon auf
upstairs oben
upstairs, to go nach oben (gehen)
upward hinauf
use Gebrauch *m.*
use, to gebrauchen, benutzen, verwenden *irr. w.*

V

valley Tal,-"er *n.*
valuables Wertsachen *pl.*
value Wert,-e *m.*
veal Kalbfleisch *n.*
very sehr, recht, ganz
vest Weste,-n *f.*
vicinity Umgebung,-en *f.*
victim Opfer,- *n.*
view Anblick,-e *m.*
vigorous tüchtig
village Dorf,-"er *n.*
vinegar Essig *m.*
visit Besuch,-e *m.*
visit, to besuchen
vow Gelübde,- *n.*
vow, to geloben
voyage Reise,-n *f.*

W

waist Taille,-n *f.*
wait, to warten
waiter Kellner,- *m.*
waiting room Wartesaal,-säle, *m.*, Wartezimmer,- *n.*
waitress Kellnerin,-nen *f.*
wake up, to aufwachen
walk, to gehen *st.v.*, zu Fuss gehen
wall (outside) Mauer,-n *f.*
waltz Walzer,- *m.*
want, to wollen
war Krieg,-e *m.*
  world . . . Weltkrieg,-e *m.*
wardrobe Garderobe,-n *f.*, Kleiderschrank,-"e *m.*
wash, to waschen *st.v.*
watch, to beobachten, aufpassen

watch Uhr,-en *f.*
watchmaker Uhrmacher,- *m.*
watch spring Uhrfeder,-n *f.*
water Wasser *n.*
wave, to winken
way Weg,-e *m.*
way back Rückweg,-e *m.*
way through Durchgang,-"e *m.*
wealth Reichtum,-"er *m.*
wear, to tragen *st.v.*
wear out, to abnützen
weather Wetter,- *n.*
wedding trip Hochzeitsreise,-n *f.*
Wednesday Mittwoch,-e *m.*
weed Unkraut,- *n.*
week Woche,-n *f.*
welcome willkommen
welcome, you are bitte (*after* danke)
well gut, wohl
  as . . . as sowie
west Westen *m.*
what was
  of . . . worüber
when wann, *int.*, als *conj.*, wenn *conj.*
whence woher
where wo
  . . . to wohin
whereupon woraufhin
whether ob
which das, welch
while während *conj.*, indem
while Weile,-n *f.*
whisper, to flüstern
whistle Pfeife,-n *f.*
white weiss
who wer *int.*, der *rel.pro.*
whoever wer
why wieso, warum, weshalb
wide breit, weit
wife Frau,-en *f.* Gemahlin,-nen *f.*
will Wille,-ns,-n *m.*
wind (watch), to aufziehen
wind Wind,-e *m.*
winding krumm
window Fenster,- *n.*
wine Wein,-e *m.*
winged beschwingt
winter Winter,- *m.*
wisdom Weisheit *f.*
wish, to wünschen, wollen

with mit
within innerhalb
without ohne
woman Frau,-en *f.*
wonder Wunder,- *n.*
wonderful wunderbar
word Wort,-"er *n.*
work Arbeit,-en *f.*
work, to arbeiten
work of art Kunstwerk,-e *n.*
works Werk,-e *n.*
   ... of a watch Uhrwerk,-e *n.*
workshop Werkstatt,-"en *f.*
world Welt,-en *f.*
worn down schiefgetreten
worry, to sorgen
worth Wert,-e *m.*
worth the money preiswert
wrist watch Armbanduhr,-en *f.*
write, to schreiben *st.v.*

write down, to aufschreiben *st.v.*
write shorthand, to stenographieren
wrong verkehrt
   to be ... (watch) falsch gehen

X Y Z

X-ray photograph
   Röntgenaufnahme,-n *f.*
year Jahr,-e *n.*
yes ja
yesterday gestern
   day before ... vorgestern
yet noch, doch
yonder drüben
young jung
youth (period of life) Jugend,- *f.*
youth (person) Junge,-n *m.*
your health! Prosit (Prost)!
zoo Zoo,- *m.*